International Instruments related to the Prevention and Suppression of International Terrorism

UNITED NATIONS

New York, 2001

ISBN: 1732952

UNITED NATIONS PUBLICATION

Sales No. E.01.V.3

ISBN 92-1-133631-7

UN 2
ST/ESA/269

CONTENTS

Part III - United Nations Declarations

Part IV - Other Instruments

PREFACE

Terrorism strikes at the very heart of everything the United Nations stands for. It presents a global threat to democracy, the rule of law, human rights and stability. Globalization brings home to us the importance of a truly concerted international effort to combat terrorism in all its forms and manifestations.

An important part of that effort is the work of the United Nations in the establishment of the necessary legal framework for the prevention and suppression of terrorism. The "treaty-making" process, covering various aspects of terrorism, has led to the adoption of many instruments over the past four decades. They have included global treaties and declarations aimed at combating international terrorism and covering a wide range of activities. Regional initiatives have also led to the adoption of regional treaties.

These instruments not only contribute to the existing jurisprudence, but also serve as a basis for the elaboration of further instruments. They give effect to the will of the Member States of the United Nations and to their unequivocal condemnation of all acts, methods and practices of terrorism as criminal and unjustifiable -- whoever commits them and wherever they occur.

The publication of this compilation of global and regional instruments on terrorism is therefore a timely testament to the commendable achievements of the international community and the unique role played by the United Nations in the fight against terrorism. As we strive to make this an age built firmly on the principles of democracy, human rights and international law, it is my hope that this publication will encourage States to become parties to those instruments to which they are not yet party. It will also give the international community a reference point for reflection on how we can further strengthen our efforts to combat terrorism in all its forms and manifestations.

Kofi A. Annan

INTRODUCTION

The General Assembly in its Declaration on Measures to Eliminate International Terrorism, annexed to resolution 49/60 of 9 December 1994, invited the United Nations, relevant specialized agencies and intergovernmental organizations and other relevant bodies to make every effort with a view to promoting measures to combat and eliminate acts of terrorism and to strengthen their role in this field.

The General Assembly, in resolution 51/210 of 17 December 1996, established an Ad Hoc Committee to elaborate legal instruments dealing with the prevention and suppression of international terrorism. The work of the Ad Hoc Committee has resulted so far in the adoption by the General Assembly of the International Convention for the Suppression of Terrorism Bombings in 1997, and the Convention for the Suppression of the Financing of Terrorism in 1999. Pursuant to resolution 54/110, the Ad Hoc Committee shall, *inter alia,* continue to elaborate a draft international convention for the suppression of nuclear terrorism and address means of further developing a comprehensive legal framework of conventions dealing with international terrorism, including considering the elaboration of a comprehensive convention on international terrorism.

This compilation of instruments related to the prevention and suppression of international terrorism is intended for use as general reference material. It is divided into four parts. Part I contains universal treaties relating to the prevention and suppression of international terrorism. Part II includes instruments adopted at the regional level. Part III includes two United Nations declarations which have provided the legal framework for international action on the prevention and suppression of terrorism in recent years. Part IV includes some relevant international treaties, or parts thereof, namely the Convention on the Safety of United Nations and Associated Personnel, adopted by the United Nations General Assembly in 1994, which has increasingly been regarded as an important instrument in the field, and the 1949 Geneva Conventions and the 1977 Protocols Additional to the Geneva Conventions.

This publication is not an exhaustive collection. It does not contain other relevant instruments, such as bilateral treaties, on the subject matter and instruments concerned with other forms of criminality, including drug trafficking, the illegal arms trade, smuggling, money laundering and organized crime.

Information relating to the status of multilateral treaties deposited with the Secretary-General of the United Nations, and information on their entry into force, can be obtained from the web site of the United Nations Treaty Collection (http://untreaty.un.org/). Access to the site is by subscription, except for certain categories of users, including, Member States, Permanent Missions, UN agencies and field offices, etc. In addition, the Secretary-General presents an annual report to the General Assembly on Measures to eliminate international terrorism, containing, *inter alia*, a detailed list of information relating to the status of all the treaties reproduced in Parts I and II of this publication. Those reports are available in electronic format at the web site of the Sixth Committee of the General Assembly (http://www.un.org/law/cod/sixth/index.html). The most recent report was issued at the fifty-fifth session of the General Assembly, in 2000, under the symbol A/55/179 and Add.1.

The present publication, which was prepared by the Codification Division of the Office of Legal Affairs of the United Nations, will also be published in French and Spanish, in separate volumes.

New York
November 2000

PART I

UNIVERSAL INSTRUMENTS

1. Convention on Offences and Certain Other Acts Committed on Board Aircraft

Signed at Tokyo on 14 September 1963
In force on 4 December 1969
United Nations, Treaty Series, vol. 704, No. 10106
Depositary: International Civil Aviation Organization

The States Parties to this Convention

Have agreed as follows:

CHAPTER I
SCOPE OF THE CONVENTION

Article 1

1. This Convention shall apply in respect of:

(*a*)   offences against penal law;

(*b*)   acts which, whether or not they are offences, may or do jeopardize the safety of the aircraft or of persons or property therein or which jeopardize good order and discipline on board.

2. Except as provided in Chapter III, this Convention shall apply in respect of offences committed or acts done by a person on board any aircraft registered in a Contracting State, while that aircraft is in flight or on the surface of the high seas or of any other area outside the territory of any State.

3. For the purposes of this Convention, an aircraft is considered to be in flight from the moment when power is applied for the purpose of take-off until the moment when the landing run ends.

4. This Convention shall not apply to aircraft used in military, customs or police services.

2

Article 2

Without prejudice to the provisions of Article 4 and except when the safety of the aircraft or of persons or property on board so requires, no provision of this Convention shall be interpreted as authorizing or requiring any action in respect of offences against penal laws of a political nature or those based on racial or religious discrimination.

CHAPTER III
JURISDICTION

Article 3

1. The State of registration of the aircraft is competent to exercise jurisdiction over offences and acts committed on board.

2. Each Contracting State shall take such measures as may be necessary to establish its jurisdiction as the State of registration over offences committed on board aircraft registered in such State.

3. This Convention does not exclude any criminal jurisdiction exercised in accordance with national law.

Article 4

A Contracting State which is not the State of registration may not interfere with an aircraft in flight in order to exercise its criminal jurisdiction over an offence committed on board except in the following cases:

(*a*)   the offence has effect on the territory of such State;

(*b*)   the offence has been committed by or against a national or permanent resident of such State;

(*c*)   the offence is against the security of such State;

(*d*)   the offence consists of a breach of any rules or regulations relating to the flight or manoeuvre of aircraft in force in such State;

(*e*)   the exercise of jurisdiction is necessary to ensure the observance of any obligation of such State under a multilateral international agreement.

CHAPTER III
POWERS OF THE AIRCRAFT COMMANDER

Article 5

1. The provisions of this Chapter shall not apply to offences and acts committed or about to be committed by a person on board an aircraft in flight in the airspace of the State of registration or over the high seas or any other area outside the territory of any State unless the last point of take-off or the next point of intended landing is situated in a State other than that of registration, or the aircraft subsequently flies in the airspace of a State other than that of registration with such person still on board.

2. Notwithstanding the provisions of Article 1, paragraph 3, an aircraft shall for the purposes of this Chapter, be considered to be in flight at any time from the moment when all its external doors are closed following embarkation until the moment when any such door is opened for disembarkation. In the case of a forced landing, the provisions of this Chapter shall continue to apply with respect to offences and acts committed on board until competent authorities of a State take over the responsibility for the aircraft and for the persons and property on board.

Article 6

1. The aircraft commander may, when he has reasonable grounds to believe that a person has committed, or is about to commit, on board the aircraft, an offence or act contemplated in Article 1, paragraph 1, impose upon such person reasonable measures including restraint which are necessary:

(*a*)   to protect the safety of the aircraft, or of persons or property therein; or

(*b*)   to maintain good order and discipline on board; or

(*c*)   to enable him to deliver such person to competent authorities or to

4

disembark him in accordance with the provisions of this Chapter.

2. The aircraft commander may require or authorize the assistance of other crew members and may request or authorize, but not require, the assistance of passengers to restrain any person whom he is entitled to restrain. Any crew member or passenger may also take reasonable preventive measures without such authorization when he has reasonable grounds to believe that such action is immediately necessary to protect the safety of the aircraft, or of persons or property therein.

Article 7

1. Measures of restraint imposed upon a person in accordance with Article 6 shall not be continued beyond any point at which the aircraft lands unless:

(*a*)   such point is in the territory of a non-Contracting State and its authorities refuse to permit disembarkation of that person or those measures have been imposed in accordance with Article 6, paragraph 1(*c*) in order to enable his delivery to competent authorities;

(*b*)   the aircraft makes a forced landing and the aircraft commander is unable to deliver that person to competent authorities; or

(*c*)   that person agrees to onward carriage under restraint.

2. The aircraft commander shall as soon as practicable, and if possible before landing in the territory of a State with a person on board who has been placed under restraint in accordance with the provisions of Article 6, notify the authorities of such State of the fact that a person on board is under restraint and of the reasons for such restraint.

Article 8

1. The aircraft commander may, in so far as it is necessary for the purpose of subparagraph (*a*) or (*b*) of paragraph 1 of Article 6, disembark in the territory of any State in which the aircraft lands any person who he has reasonable grounds to believe has committed, or is about to commit, on board the aircraft an act contemplated in Article 1, paragraph 1(*b*).

2. The aircraft commander shall report to the authorities of the State in which he disembarks any person pursuant to this Article, the fact of, and the reasons for, such disembarkation.

Article 9

1. The aircraft commander may deliver to the competent authorities of any Contracting State in the territory of which the aircraft lands any person who he has reasonable grounds to believe has committed on board the aircraft an act which, in his opinion, is a serious offence according to the penal law of the State of registration of the aircraft.

2. The aircraft commander shall as soon as practicable and if possible before landing in the territory of a Contracting State with a person on board whom the aircraft commander intends to deliver in accordance with the preceding paragraph, notify the authorities of such State of his intention to deliver such person and the reasons therefor.

3. The aircraft commander shall furnish the authorities to whom any suspected offender is delivered in accordance with the provisions of this Article with evidence and information which, under the law of the State of registration of the aircraft, are lawfully in his possession.

Article 10

For actions taken in accordance with this Convention, neither the aircraft commander, any other member of the crew, any passenger, the owner or operator of the aircraft, nor the person on whose behalf the flight was performed shall be held responsible in any proceeding on account of the treatment undergone by the person against whom the actions were taken.

CHAPTER IV
UNLAWFUL SEIZURE OF AIRCRAFT

Article 11

1. When a person on board has unlawfully committed by force or threat thereof an act of interference, seizure, or other wrongful exercise of control of an aircraft in flight or when such an act is about to be

committed, Contracting States shall take all appropriate measures to restore control of the aircraft to its lawful commander or to preserve his control of the aircraft.

2. In the cases contemplated in the preceding paragraph, the Contracting State in which the aircraft lands shall permit its passengers and crew to continue their journey as soon as practicable, and shall return the aircraft and its cargo to the persons lawfully entitled to possession.

CHAPTER V
POWERS AND DUTIES OF STATES

Article 12

Any Contracting State shall allow the commander of an aircraft registered in another Contracting State to disembark any person pursuant to Article 8, paragraph 1.

Article 13

1. Any Contracting State shall take delivery of any person whom the aircraft commander delivers pursuant to Article 9, paragraph 1.

2. Upon being satisfied that the circumstances so warrant, any Contracting State shall take custody or other measures to ensure the presence of any person suspected of an act contemplated in Article 11, paragraph 1 and of any person of whom it has taken delivery. The custody and other measures shall be as provided in the law of that State but may only be continued for such time as is reasonably necessary to enable any criminal or extradition proceedings to be instituted.

3. Any person in custody pursuant to the previous paragraph shall be assisted in communicating immediately with the nearest appropriate representative of the State of which he is a national.

4. Any Contracting State, to which a person is delivered pursuant to Article 9, paragraph 1, or in whose territory an aircraft lands following the commission of an act contemplated in Article 11, paragraph 1, shall immediately make a preliminary enquiry into the facts.

7

5. When a State, pursuant to this Article, has taken a person into custody, it shall immediately notify the State of registration of the aircraft and the State of nationality of the detained person and, if it considers it advisable, any other interested State of the fact that such person is in custody and of the circumstances which warrant his detention. The State which makes the preliminary enquiry contemplated in paragraph 4 of this Article shall promptly report its findings to the said States and shall indicate whether it intends to exercise jurisdiction.

Article 14

1. When any person has been disembarked in accordance with Article 8, paragraph 1, or delivered in accordance with Article 9, paragraph 1, or has disembarked after committing an act contemplated in Article 11, paragraph 1, and when such person cannot or does not desire to continue his journey and the State of landing refuses to admit him, that State may, if the person in question is not a national or permanent resident of that State, return him to the territory of the State of which he is a national or permanent resident or to the territory of the State in which he began his journey by air.

2. Neither disembarkation, nor delivery, nor the taking of custody or other measures contemplated in Article 13, paragraph 2, nor return of the person concerned, shall be considered as admission to the territory of the Contracting State concerned for the purpose of its law relating to entry or admission of persons and nothing in this Convention shall affect the law of a Contracting State relating to the expulsion of persons from its territory.

Article 15

1. Without prejudice to Article 14, any person who has been disembarked in accordance with Article 8, paragraph 1, or delivered in accordance with Article 9, paragraph 1, or has disembarked after committing an act contemplated in Article 11, paragraph 1, and who desires to continue his journey shall be at liberty as soon as practicable to proceed to any destination of his choice unless his presence is required by the law of the State of landing for the purpose of extradition or criminal proceedings.

2. Without prejudice to its law as to entry and admission to, and extradition and expulsion from its territory, a Contracting State in whose territory a person has been disembarked in accordance with Article 8, paragraph 1, or delivered in accordance with Article 9, paragraph 1 or has disembarked and is suspected of having committed an act contemplated in Article 11, paragraph 1, shall accord to such person treatment which is no less favourable for his protection and security than that accorded to nationals of such Contracting State in like circumstances.

CHAPTER VI
OTHER PROVISIONS

Article 16

1. Offences committed on aircraft registered in a Contracting State shall be treated, for the purpose of extradition, as if they had been committed not only in the place in which they have occurred but also in the territory of the State of registration of the aircraft.

2. Without prejudice to the provisions of the preceding paragraph, nothing in this Convention shall be deemed to create an obligation to grant extradition.

Article 17

In taking any measures for investigation or arrest or otherwise exercising jurisdiction in connection with any offence committed on board an aircraft the Contracting States shall pay due regard to the safety and other interests of air navigation and shall so act as to avoid unnecessary delay of the aircraft, passengers, crew or cargo.

Article 18

If Contracting States establish joint air transport operating organizations or international operating agencies, which operate aircraft not registered in any one State those States shall, according to the circumstances of the case, designate the State among them which, for the purposes of this Convention, shall be considered as the State of registration and shall give notice thereof to the International Civil Aviation Organization which shall communicate the notice to all States Parties to this Convention.

9

CHAPTER VII
FINAL CLAUSES

Article 19

Until the date on which this Convention comes into force in accordance with the provisions of Article 21, it shall remain open for signature on behalf of any State which at that date is a Member of the United Nations or of any of the Specialized Agencies.

Article 20

1. This Convention shall be subject to ratification by the signatory States in accordance with their constitutional procedures.

2. The instruments of ratification shall be deposited with the International Civil Aviation Organization.

Article 21

1. As soon as twelve of the signatory States have deposited their instruments of ratification of this Convention, it shall come into force between them on the ninetieth day after the date of the deposit of the twelfth instrument of ratification. It shall come into force for each State ratifying thereafter on the ninetieth day after the deposit of its instrument of ratification.

2. As soon as this Convention comes into force, it shall be registered with the Secretary-General of the United Nations by the International Civil Aviation Organization.

Article 22

1. This Convention shall, after it has come into force, be open for accession by any State Member of the United Nations or of any of the Specialized Agencies.

2. The accession of a State shall be effected by the deposit of an instrument of accession with the International Civil Aviation Organization and shall take effect on the ninetieth day after the date of such deposit.

Article 23

1. Any Contracting State may denounce this Convention by notification addressed to the International Civil Aviation Organization.

2. Denunciation shall take effect six months after the date of receipt by the International Civil Aviation Organization of the notification of denunciation.

Article 24

1. Any dispute between two or more Contracting States concerning the interpretation or application of this Convention which cannot be settled through negotiation, shall, at the request of one of them, be submitted to arbitration. If within six months from the date of the request for arbitration the Parties are unable to agree on the organization of the arbitration, any one of those Parties may refer the dispute to the International Court of Justice by request in conformity with the Statute of the Court.

2. Each State may at the time of signature or ratification of this Convention or accession thereto, declare that it does not consider itself bound by the preceding paragraph. The other Contracting States shall not be bound by the preceding paragraph with respect to any Contracting State having made such a reservation.

3. Any Contracting State having made a reservation in accordance with the preceding paragraph may at any time withdraw this reservation by notification to the International Civil Aviation Organization.

Article 25

Except as provided in Article 24 no reservation may be made to this Convention.

Article 26

The International Civil Aviation Organization shall give notice to all States Members of the United Nations or of any of the Specialized Agencies:

(*a*)   of any signature of this Convention and the date thereof;

(*b*)   of the deposit of any instrument of ratification or accession and the date thereof;

(*c*)   of the date on which this Convention comes into force in accordance with Article 21, paragraph 1;

(*d*)   of the receipt of any notification of denunciation and the date thereof; and

(*e*)   of the receipt of any declaration or notification made under Article 24 and the date thereof.

IN WITNESS WHEREOF the undersigned Plenipotentiaries, having been duly authorized, have signed this Convention.

DONE at Tokyo on the fourteenth day of September, One Thousand Nine Hundred and Sixty-three in three authentic texts drawn up in the English, French and Spanish languages.

This Convention shall be deposited with the International Civil Aviation Organization with which, in accordance with Article 19, it shall remain open for signature and the said Organization shall send certified copies thereof to all States Members of the United Nations or of any Specialized Agency.

————————————

2. Convention for the Suppression of Unlawful Seizure of Aircraft

Signed at The Hague on 16 December 1970
In force on 14 October 1971
United Nations, Treaty Series, vol. 860, No. 12325
Depositary: Russian Federation, United Kingdom of Great Britain and
Northern Ireland and the United States of America

Preamble

The States Parties to this Convention

CONSIDERING that unlawful acts of seizure or exercise of control of aircraft in flight jeopardize the safety of persons and property, seriously affect the operation of air services, and undermine the confidence of the peoples of the world in the safety of civil aviation;

CONSIDERING that the occurrence of such acts is a matter of grave concern;

CONSIDERING that, for the purpose of deterring such acts, there is an urgent need to provide appropriate measures for punishment of offenders;

Have agreed as follows:

Article 1

Any person who on board an aircraft in flight:

(*a*)   unlawfully, by force or threat thereof, or by any other form of intimidation, seizes, or exercises control of, that aircraft, or attempts to perform any such act, or

(*b*)   is an accomplice of a person who performs or attempts to perform any such act commits an offence (hereinafter referred to as "the offence").

Article 2

Each Contracting State undertakes to make the offence punishable by severe penalties.

Article 3

1. For the purposes of this Convention, an aircraft is considered to be in flight at any time from the moment when all its external doors are closed following embarkation until the moment when any such door is opened for disembarkation. In the case of a forced landing, the flight shall be deemed to continue until the competent authorities take over the responsibility for the aircraft and for persons and property on board.

2. This Convention shall not apply to aircraft used in military, customs or police services.

3. This Convention shall apply only if the place of take-off or the place of actual landing of the aircraft on board which the offence is committed is situated outside the territory of the State of registration of that aircraft; it shall be immaterial whether the aircraft is engaged in an international or domestic flight.

4. In the cases mentioned in Article 5, this Convention shall not apply if the place of take-off and the place of actual landing of the aircraft on board which the offence is committed are situated within the territory of the same State where that State is one of those referred to in that Article.

5. Notwithstanding paragraphs 3 and 4 of this Article, Articles 6, 7, 8 and 10 shall apply whatever the place of take-off or the place of actual landing of the aircraft, if the offender or the alleged offender is found in the territory of a State other than the State of registration of that aircraft.

Article 4

1. Each Contracting State shall take such measures as may be necessary to establish its jurisdiction over the offence and any other act of

violence against passengers or crew committed by the alleged offender in connection with the offence, in the following cases:

(*a*)   when the offence is committed on board an aircraft registered in that State;

(*b*)   when the aircraft on board which the offence is committed lands in its territory with the alleged offender still on board;

(*c*)   when the offence is committed on board an aircraft leased without crew to a lessee who has his principal place of business or, if the lessee has no such place of business, his permanent residence, in that State.

2. Each Contracting State shall likewise take such measures as may be necessary to establish its jurisdiction over the offence in the case where the alleged offender is present in its territory and it does not extradite him pursuant to Article 8 to any of the States mentioned in paragraph 1 of this Article.

3. This Convention does not exclude any criminal jurisdiction exercised in accordance with national law.

Article 5

The Contracting States which establish joint air transport operating organizations or international operating agencies, which operate aircraft which are subject to joint or international registration shall, by appropriate means, designate for each aircraft the State among them which shall exercise the jurisdiction and have the attributes of the State of registration for the purpose of this Convention and shall give notice thereof to the International Civil Aviation Organization which shall communicate the notice to all States Parties to this Convention.

Article 6

1. Upon being satisfied that the circumstances so warrant, any Contracting State in the territory of which the offender or the alleged offender is present, shall take him into custody or take other measures to ensure his presence. The custody and other measures shall be as provided

in the law of that State but may only be continued for such time as is necessary to enable any criminal or extradition proceedings to be instituted.

2. Such State shall immediately make a preliminary enquiry into the facts.

3. Any person in custody pursuant to paragraph 1 of this Article shall be assisted in communicating immediately with the nearest appropriate representative of the State of which he is a national.

4. When a State, pursuant to this Article, has taken a person into custody, it shall immediately notify the State of registration of the aircraft, the State mentioned in Article 4, paragraph 1(*c*), the State of nationality of the detained person and, if it considers it advisable, any other interested States of the fact that such person is in custody and of the circumstances which warrant his detention. The State which makes the preliminary enquiry contemplated in paragraph 2 of this Article shall promptly report its findings to the said States and shall indicate whether it intends to exercise jurisdiction.

Article 7

The Contracting State in the territory of which the alleged offender is found shall, if it does not extradite him, be obliged, without exception whatsoever and whether or not the offence was committed in its territory, to submit the case to its competent authorities for the purpose of prosecution. Those authorities shall take their decision in the same manner as in the case of any ordinary offence of a serious nature under the law of that State.

Article 8

1. The offence shall be deemed to be included as an extraditable offence in any extradition treaty existing between Contracting States. Contracting States undertake to include the offence as an extraditable offence in every extradition treaty to be concluded between them.

2. If a Contracting State which makes extradition conditional on the existence of a treaty receives a request for extradition from another

Contracting State with which it has no extradition treaty, it may at its option consider this Convention as the legal basis for extradition in respect of the offence. Extradition shall be subject to the other conditions provided by the law of the requested State.

3. Contracting States which do not make extradition conditional on the existence of a treaty shall recognize the offence as an extraditable offence between themselves subject to the conditions provided by the law of the requested State.

4. The offence shall be treated, for the purpose of extradition between Contracting States, as if it had been committed not only in the place in which it occurred but also in the territories of the States required to establish their jurisdiction in accordance with Article 4, paragraph 1.

Article 9

1. When any of the acts mentioned in Article 1(*a*) has occurred or is about to occur, Contracting States shall take all appropriate measures to restore control of the aircraft to its lawful commander or to preserve his control of the aircraft.

2. In the cases contemplated by the preceding paragraph, any Contracting State in which the aircraft or its passengers or crew are present shall facilitate the continuation of the journey of the passengers and crew as soon as practicable, and shall without delay return the aircraft and its cargo to the persons lawfully entitled to possession.

Article 10

1. Contracting States shall afford one another the greatest measure of assistance in connection with criminal proceedings brought in respect of the offence and other acts mentioned in Article 4. The law of the State requested shall apply in all cases.

2. The provisions of paragraph 1 of this Article shall not affect obligations under any other treaty, bilateral or multilateral, which governs or will govern, in whole or in part, mutual assistance in criminal matters.

Article 11

Each Contracting State shall in accordance with its national law report to the Council of the International Civil Aviation Organization as promptly as possible any relevant information in its possession concerning:

(*a*)   the circumstances of the offence;

(*b*)   the action taken pursuant to Article 9;

(*c*)   the measures taken in relation to the offender or the alleged offender, and, in particular, the results of any extradition proceedings or other legal proceedings.

Article 12

1. Any dispute between two or more Contracting States concerning the interpretation or application of this Convention which cannot be settled through negotiation, shall, at the request of one of them, be submitted to arbitration. If within six months from the date of the request for arbitration the Parties are unable to agree on the organization of the arbitration, any one of those Parties may refer the dispute to the International Court of Justice by request in conformity with the Statute of the Court.

2. Each State may at the time of signature or ratification of this Convention or accession thereto, declare that it does not consider itself bound by the preceding paragraph. The other Contracting States shall not be bound by the preceding paragraph with respect to any Contracting State having made such a reservation.

3. Any Contracting State having made a reservation in accordance with the preceding paragraph may at any time withdraw this reservation by notification to the Depositary Governments.

Article 13

1. This Convention shall be open for signature at The Hague on 16 December 1970, by States participating in the International Conference on Air Law held at The Hague from 1 to 16 December 1970 (hereinafter

referred to as The Hague Conference). After 31 December 1970, the Convention shall be open to all States for signature in Moscow, London and Washington. Any State which does not sign this Convention before its entry into force in accordance with paragraph 3 of this Article may accede to it at any time.

2. This Convention shall be subject to ratification by the signatory States. Instruments of ratification and instruments of accession shall be deposited with the Governments of the Union of Soviet Socialist Republics, the United Kingdom of Great Britain and Northern Ireland, and the United States of America, which are hereby designated the Depositary Governments.

3. This Convention shall enter into force thirty days following the date of the deposit of instruments of ratification by ten States signatory to this Convention which participated in The Hague Conference.

4. For other States, this Convention shall enter into force on the date of entry into force of this Convention in accordance with paragraph 3 of this Article, or thirty days following the date of deposit of their instruments of ratification or accession, whichever is later.

5. The Depositary Governments shall promptly inform all signatory and acceding States of the date of each signature, the date of deposit of each instrument of ratification or accession, the date of entry into force of this Convention, and other notices.

6. As soon as this Convention comes into force, it shall be registered by the Depositary Governments pursuant to Article 102 of the Charter of the United Nations and pursuant to Article 83 of the Convention on International Civil Aviation (Chicago, 1944).

Article 14

1. Any Contracting State may denounce this Convention by written notification to the Depositary Governments.

2. Denunciation shall take effect six months following the date on which notification is received by the Depositary Governments.

IN WITNESS WHEREOF the undersigned Plenipotentiaries, being duly authorised thereto by their Governments, have signed this Convention.

DONE at The Hague, this sixteenth day of December, one thousand nine hundred and seventy, in three originals, each being drawn up in four authentic texts in the English, French, Russian and Spanish languages.

3. Convention for the Suppression of Unlawful Acts against the Safety of Civil Aviation

Concluded at Montreal on 23 September 1971
In force on 26 January 1973
United Nations, Treaty Series, vol. 974, No. 14118
Depositary: Russian Federation, United Kingdom of Great Britain and Northern Ireland and the United States of America

The States Parties to the Convention

CONSIDERING that unlawful acts against the safety of civil aviation jeopardize the safety of persons and property, seriously affect the operation of air services, and undermine the confidence of the peoples of the world in the safety of civil aviation;

CONSIDERING that the occurrence of such acts is a matter of grave concern;

CONSIDERING that, for the purpose of deterring such acts, there is an urgent need to provide appropriate measures for punishment of offenders;

Have agreed as follows:

Article 1

1. Any person commits an offence if he unlawfully and intentionally:

(a)   performs an act of violence against a person on board an aircraft in flight if that act is likely to endanger the safety of that aircraft; or

(b)   destroys an aircraft in service or causes damage to such an aircraft which renders it incapable of flight or which is likely to endanger its safety in flight; or

(c)   places or causes to be placed on an aircraft in service, by any means whatsoever, a device or substance which is likely to destroy that aircraft, or to cause damage to it which renders it incapable of flight, or to cause damage to it which is likely to endanger its safety in flight; or

(d)   destroys or damages air navigation facilities or interferes with their operation, if any such act is likely to endanger the safety of aircraft in flight; or

(e)   communicates information which he knows to be false, thereby endangering the safety of an aircraft in flight.

2. Any person also commits an offence if he:

(a)   attempts to commit any of the offences mentioned in paragraph 1 of this Article; or

(b)   is an accomplice of a person who commits or attempts to commit any such offence.

Article 2

For the purposes of this Convention:

(a)   an aircraft is considered to be in flight at any time from the moment when all its external doors are closed following embarkation until the moment when any such door is opened for disembarkation; in the case of a forced landing, the flight shall be deemed to continue until the competent authorities take over the responsibility for the aircraft and for persons and property on board;

(b)   an aircraft is considered to be in service from the beginning of the preflight preparation of the aircraft by ground personnel or by the crew for a specific flight until twenty-four hours after any landing; the period of service shall, in any event, extend for the entire period during which the aircraft is in flight as defined in paragraph (a) of this Article.

Article 3

Each Contracting State undertakes to make the offences mentioned in Article 1 punishable by severe penalties.

Article 4

1. This Convention shall not apply to aircraft used in military, customs or police services.

2. In the cases contemplated in subparagraphs (*a*), (*b*), (*c*) and (*e*) of paragraph 1 of Article 1, this Convention shall apply, irrespective of whether the aircraft is engaged in an international or domestic flight, only if:

(*a*) the place of take-off or landing, actual or intended, of the aircraft is situated outside the territory of the State of registration of that aircraft; or

(*b*) the offence is committed in the territory of a State other than the State of registration of the aircraft.

3. Notwithstanding paragraph 2 of this Article, in the cases contemplated in subparagraphs (*a*), (*b*), (*c*) and (*e*) of paragraph 1 of Article 1, this Convention shall also apply if the offender or the alleged offender is found in the territory of a State other than the State of registration of the aircraft.

4. With respect to the States mentioned in Article 9 and in the cases mentioned in subparagraphs (*a*), (*b*), (*c*) and (*e*) of paragraph 1 of Article 1, this Convention shall not apply if the places referred to in subparagraph (*a*) of paragraph 2 of this Article are situated within the territory of the same State where that State is one of those referred to in Article 9, unless the offence is committed or the offender or alleged offender is found in the territory of a State other than that State.

5. In the cases contemplated in subparagraph (*d*) of paragraph 1 of Article 1, this Convention shall apply only if the air navigation facilities are used in international air navigation.

6. The provisions of paragraphs 2, 3, 4 and 5 of this Article shall also apply in the cases contemplated in paragraph 2 of Article 1.

Article 5

1. Each Contracting State shall take such measures as may be necessary to establish its jurisdiction over the offences in the following cases:

(a)   when the offence is committed in the territory of that State;

(b)   when the offence is committed against or on board an aircraft registered in that State;

(c)   when the aircraft on board which the offence is committed lands in its territory with the alleged offender still on board;

(d)   when the offence is committed against or on board an aircraft leased without crew to a lessee who has his principal place of business or, if the lessee has no such place of business, his permanent residence, in that State.

2. Each Contracting State shall likewise take such measures as may be necessary to establish its jurisdiction over the offences mentioned in Article 1, paragraph 1 (a), (b) and (c), and in Article 1, paragraph 2, in so far as that paragraph relates to those offences, in the case where the alleged offender is present in its territory and it does not extradite him pursuant to Article 8 to any of the States mentioned in paragraph 1 of this Article.

3. This Convention does not exclude any criminal jurisdiction exercised in accordance with national law.

Article 6

1. Upon being satisfied that the circumstances so warrant, any Contracting State in the territory of which the offender or the alleged offender is present, shall take him into custody or take other measures to ensure his presence. The custody and other measures shall be as provided in the law of that State but may only be continued for such time as is

necessary to enable any criminal or extradition proceedings to be instituted.

2. Such State shall immediately make a preliminary enquiry into the facts.

3. Any person in custody pursuant to paragraph 1 of this Article shall be assisted in communicating immediately with the nearest appropriate representative of the State of which he is a national.

4. When a State, pursuant to this Article, has taken a person into custody, it shall immediately notify the States mentioned in Article 5, paragraph 1, the State of nationality of the detained person and, if it considers it advisable, any other interested State of the fact that such person is in custody and of the circumstances which warrant his detention. The State which makes the preliminary enquiry contemplated in paragraph 2 of this Article shall promptly report its findings to the said States and shall indicate whether it intends to exercise jurisdiction.

Article 7

The Contracting State in the territory of which the alleged offender is found shall, if it does not extradite him, be obliged, without exception whatsoever and whether or not the offence was committed in its territory, to submit the case to its competent authorities for the purpose of prosecution. Those authorities shall take their decision in the same manner as in the case of any ordinary offence of a serious nature under the law of that State.

Article 8

1. The offences shall be deemed to be included as extraditable offences in any extradition treaty existing between Contracting States. Contracting States undertake to include the offences as extraditable offences in every extradition treaty to be concluded between them.

2. If a Contracting State which makes extradition conditional on the existence of a treaty receives a request for extradition from another Contracting State with which it has no extradition treaty, it may at its option consider this Convention as the legal basis for extradition in respect

of the offences. Extradition shall be subject to the other conditions provided by the law of the requested State.

3. Contracting States which do not make extradition conditional on the existence of a treaty shall recognize the offences as extraditable offences between themselves subject to the conditions provided by the law of the requested State.

4. Each of the offences shall be treated, for the purpose of extradition between Contracting States, as if it had been committed not only in the place in which it occurred but also in the territories of the States required to establish their jurisdiction in accordance with Article 5, paragraph 1 (*b*), (*c*) and (*d*).

Article 9

The Contracting States which establish joint air transport operating organizations or international operating agencies, which operate aircraft which are subject to joint or international registration shall, by appropriate means, designate for each aircraft the State among them which shall exercise the jurisdiction and have the attributes of the State of registration for the purpose of this Convention and shall give notice thereof to the International Civil Aviation Organization which shall communicate the notice to all States Parties to this Convention.

Article 10

1. Contracting States shall, in accordance with international and national law, endeavour to take all practicable measure for the purpose of preventing the offences mentioned in Article 1.

2. When, due to the commission of one of the offences mentioned in Article 1, a flight has been delayed or interrupted, any Contracting State in whose territory the aircraft or passengers or crew are present shall facilitate the continuation of the journey of the passengers and crew as soon as practicable, and shall without delay return the aircraft and its cargo to the persons lawfully entitled to possession.

Article 11

1. Contracting States shall afford one another the greatest measure of assistance in connection with criminal proceedings brought in respect of the offences. The law of the State requested shall apply in all cases.

2. The provisions of paragraph 1 of this Article shall not affect obligations under any other treaty, bilateral or multilateral, which governs or will govern, in whole or in part, mutual assistance in criminal matters.

Article 12

Any Contracting State having reason to believe that one of the offences mentioned in Article 1 will be committed shall, in accordance with its national law, furnish any relevant information in its possession to those States which it believes would be the States mentioned in Article 5, paragraph 1.

Article 13

Each Contracting State shall in accordance with its national law report to the Council of the International Civil Aviation Organization as promptly as possible any relevant information in its possession concerning:

(*a*)   the circumstances of the offence;

(*b*)   the action taken pursuant to Article 10, paragraph 2;

(*c*)   the measures taken in relation to the offender or the alleged offender and, in particular, the results of any extradition proceedings or other legal proceedings.

Article 14

1. Any dispute between two or more Contracting States concerning the interpretation or application of this Convention which cannot be settled through negotiation, shall, at the request of one of them, be submitted to arbitration. If within six months from the date of the request for arbitration the Parties are unable to agree on the organization of the arbitration, any

one of those Parties may refer the dispute to the International Court of Justice by request in conformity with the Statute of the Court.

2. Each State may at the time of signature or ratification of this Convention or accession thereto, declare that it does not consider itself bound by the preceding paragraph. The other Contracting States shall not be bound by the preceding paragraph with respect to any Contracting State having made such a reservation.

3. Any Contracting State having made a reservation in accordance with the preceding paragraph may at any time withdraw this reservation by notification to the Depositary Governments.

Article 15

1. This Convention shall be open for signature at Montreal on 23 September 1971, by States participating in the International Conference on Air Law held at Montreal from 8 to 23 September 1971 (hereinafter referred to as the Montreal Conference). After 10 October 1971, the Convention shall be open to all States for signature in Moscow, London and Washington. Any State which does not sign this Convention before its entry into force in accordance with paragraph 3 of this Article may accede to it at any time.

2. This Convention shall be subject to ratification by the signatory States. Instruments of ratification and instruments of accession shall be deposited with the Governments of the Union of Soviet Socialist Republics, the United Kingdom of Great Britain and Northern Ireland, and the United States of America, which are hereby designated the Depositary Governments.

3. This Convention shall enter into force thirty days following the date of the deposit of instruments of ratification by ten States signatory to this Convention which participated in the Montreal Conference.

4. For other States, this Convention shall enter into force on the date of entry into force of this Convention in accordance with paragraph 3 of this Article, or thirty days following the date of deposit of their instruments of ratification or accession, whichever is later.

5. The Depositary Governments shall promptly inform all signatory and acceding States of the date of each signature, the date of deposit of each instrument of ratification or accession, the date of entry into force of this Convention, and other notices.

6. As soon as this Convention comes into force, it shall be registered by the Depositary Governments pursuant to Article 102 of the Convention on International Civil Aviation (Chicago, 1944).

Article 16

1. Any Contracting State may denounce this Convention by written notification to the Depositary Governments.

2. Denunciation shall take effect six months following the date on which notification is received by the Depositary Governments.

IN WITNESS WHEREOF the undersigned Plenipotentiaries, being duly authorized thereto by their Governments, have signed this Convention.

DONE at Montreal, this twenty-third day of September, one thousand nine hundred and seventy-one, in three originals, each being drawn up in four authentic texts in the English, French, Russian and Spanish languages.

4. Convention on the Prevention and Punishment of Crimes against Internationally Protected Persons, including Diplomatic Agents

Adopted by the General Assembly of the United Nations on 14 December 1973
In force on 20 February 1977
United Nations, Treaty Series, vol. 1035, No. 15410
Depositary: Secretary-General of the United Nations

The States Parties to this Convention,

HAVING IN MIND the purposes and principles of the Charter of the United Nations concerning the maintenance of international peace and the promotion of friendly relations and co-operation among States,

CONSIDERING that crimes against diplomatic agents and other internationally protected persons jeopardizing the safety of these persons create a serious threat to the maintenance of normal international relations which are necessary for co-operation among States,

BELIEVING that the commission of such crimes is a matter of grave concern to the international community,

CONVINCED that there is an urgent need to adopt appropriate and effective measures for the prevention and punishment of such crimes,

Have agreed as follows:

Article 1

For the purposes of this Convention:

1. "Internationally protected person" means:

(a)   a head of State, including any member of a collegial body performing the functions of a Head of State under the constitution of the State concerned, a Head of Government or a Minister for

Foreign Affairs, whenever any such person is in a foreign State, as well as members of his family who accompany him;

(*b*)   any representative or official of a State or any official or other agent of an international organization of an intergovernmental character who, at the time when and in the place where a crime against him, his official premises, his private accommodation or his means of transport is committed, is entitled pursuant to international law to special protection from any attack on his person, freedom or dignity, as well as members of his family forming part of his household;

2. "Alleged offender" means a person as to whom there is sufficient evidence to determine *prima facie* that he has committed or participated in one or more of the crimes set forth in Article 2.

Article 2

1. The intentional commission of:

(*a*)   a murder, kidnapping or other attack upon the person or liberty of an internationally protected person;

(*b*)   a violent attack upon the official premises, the private accommodation or the means of transport of an internationally protected person likely to endanger his person or liberty;

(*c*)   a threat to commit any such attack;

(*d*)   an attempt to commit any such attack; and

(*e*)   an act constituting participation as an accomplice in any such attack;

shall be made by each State Party a crime under its internal law.

2. Each State Party shall make these crimes punishable by appropriate penalties which take into account their grave nature.

3. Paragraphs 1 and 2 of this Article in no way derogate from the

obligations of States Parties under international law to take all appropriate measures to prevent other attacks on the person, freedom or dignity of an internationally protected person.

Article 3

1. Each State Party shall take such measures as may be necessary to establish its jurisdiction over the crimes set forth in Article 2 in the following cases:

(*a*)   when the crime is committed in the territory of that State or on board a ship or aircraft registered in that State;

(*b*)   when the alleged offender is a national of that State;

(*c*)   when the crime is committed against an internationally protected person as defined in Article 1 who enjoys his status as such by virtue of functions which he exercises on behalf of that State.

2. Each State Party shall likewise take such measures as may be necessary to establish its jurisdiction over these crimes in cases where the alleged offender is present in its territory and it does not extradite him pursuant to Article 8 to any of the States mentioned in paragraph 1 of this Article.

3. This Convention does not exclude any criminal jurisdiction exercised in accordance with internal law.

Article 4

States Parties shall co-operate in the prevention of the crimes set forth in Article 2, particularly by:

(*a*)   taking all practicable measures to prevent preparations in their respective territories for the commission of those crimes within or outside their territories;

(*b*)   exchanging information and co-ordinating the taking of administrative and other measures as appropriate to prevent the commission of those crimes.

Article 5

1. The State Party in which any of the crimes set forth in Article 2 has been committed shall, if it has reason to believe that an alleged offender has fled from its territory, communicate to all other States concerned, directly or through the Secretary-General of the United Nations, all the pertinent facts regarding the crime committed and all available information regarding the identity of the alleged offender.

2. Whenever any of the crimes set forth in Article 2 has been committed against an internationally protected person, any State Party which has information concerning the victim and the circumstances of the crime shall endeavour to transmit it, under the conditions provided for in its internal law, fully and promptly to the State Party on whose behalf he was exercising his functions.

Article 6

1. Upon being satisfied that the circumstances so warrant, the State Party in whose territory the alleged offender is present shall take the appropriate measures under its internal law so as to ensure his presence for the purpose of prosecution or extradition. Such measures shall be notified without delay directly or through the Secretary-General of the United Nations to:

(*a*)   the State where the crime was committed;

(*b*)   the State or States of which the alleged offender is a national or, if he is a stateless person, in whose territory he permanently resides;

(*c*)   the State or States of which the internationally protected person concerned is a national or on whose behalf he was exercising his functions;

(*d*)   all other States concerned; and

(*e*)   the international organization of which the internationally protected person concerned is an official or an agent.

2. Any person regarding whom the measures referred to in

33

paragraph 1 of this Article are being taken shall be entitled:

(*a*)   to communicate without delay with the nearest appropriate representative of the State of which he is a national or which is otherwise entitled to protect his rights or, if he is a stateless person, which he requests and which is willing to protect his rights; and

(*b*)   to be visited by a representative of that State.

Article 7

The State Party in whose territory the alleged offender is present shall, if it does not extradite him, submit, without exception whatsoever and without undue delay, the case to its competent authorities for the purpose of prosecution, through proceedings in accordance with the laws of that State.

Article 8

1. To the extent that the crimes set forth in Article 2 are not listed as extraditable offences in any extradition treaty existing between States Parties, they shall be deemed to be included as such therein. States Parties undertake to include those crimes as extraditable offences in every future extradition treaty to be concluded between them.

2. If a State Party which makes extradition conditional on the existence of a treaty receives a request for extradition from another State Party with which it has no extradition treaty, it may, if it decides to extradite, consider this Convention as the legal basis for extradition in respect of those crimes. Extradition shall be subject to the procedural provisions and the other conditions of the law of the requested State.

3. States Parties which do not make extradition conditional on the existence of a treaty shall recognize those crimes as extraditable offences between themselves subject to the procedural provisions and the other conditions of the law of the requested State.

4. Each of the crimes shall be treated, for the purpose of extradition between States Parties, as if it had been committed not only in the place in which it occurred but also in the territories of the States required to establish their jurisdiction in accordance with paragraph 1 of Article 3.

Article 9

Any person regarding whom proceedings are being carried out in connexion with any of the crimes set forth in Article 2 shall be guaranteed fair treatment at all stages of the proceedings.

Article 10

1. States Parties shall afford one another the greatest measure of assistance in connexion with criminal proceedings brought in respect of the crimes set forth in Article 2, including the supply of all evidence at their disposal necessary for the proceedings.

2. The provisions of paragraph 1 of this Article shall not affect obligations concerning mutual judicial assistance embodied in any other treaty.

Article 11

The State Party where an alleged offender is prosecuted shall communicate the final outcome of the proceedings to the Secretary-General of the United Nations, who shall transmit the information to the other States Parties.

Article 12

The provisions of this Convention shall not affect the application of the Treaties on Asylum, in force at the date of the adoption of this Convention, as between the States which are parties to those Treaties; but a State Party to this Convention may not invoke those Treaties with respect to another State Party to this Convention which is not a party to those Treaties.

Article 13

1. Any dispute between two or more States Parties concerning the interpretation or application of this Convention which is not settled by negotiation shall, at the request of one of them, be submitted to arbitration. If within six months from the date of the request for arbitration the Parties are unable to agree on the organization of the arbitration, any one of those

Parties may refer the dispute to the International Court of Justice by request in conformity with the Statute of the Court.

2. Each State Party may at the time of signature or ratification of this Convention or accession thereto declare that it does not consider itself bound by paragraph 1 of this Article. The other States Parties shall not be bound by paragraph 1 of this Article with respect to any State Party which has made such a reservation.

3. Any State Party which has made a reservation in accordance with paragraph 2 of this Article may at any time withdraw that reservation by notification to the Secretary-General of the United Nations.

Article 14

This Convention shall be opened for signature by all States, until 31 December 1974, at United Nations Headquarters in New York.

Article 15

This Convention is subject to ratification. The instruments of ratification shall be deposited with the Secretary-General of the United Nations.

Article 16

This Convention shall remain open for accession by any State. The instruments of accession shall be deposited with the Secretary-General of the United Nations.

Article 17

1. This Convention shall enter into force on the thirtieth day following the date of deposit of the twenty-second instrument of ratification or accession with the Secretary-General of the United Nations.

2. For each State ratifying or acceding to the Convention after the deposit of the twenty-second instrument of ratification or accession, the Convention shall enter into force on the thirtieth day after deposit by such State of its instrument of ratification or accession.

Article 18

1. Any State Party may denounce this Convention by written notification to the Secretary-General of the United Nations.

2. Denunciation shall take effect six months following the date on which notification is received by the Secretary-General of the United Nations.

Article 19

The Secretary-General of the United Nations shall inform all States, *inter alia*:

(*a*)   of signatures to this Convention, of the deposit of instruments of ratification or accession in accordance with Articles 14, 15 and 16 and of notifications made under Article 18;

(*b*)   of the date on which this Convention will enter into force in accordance with Article 17.

Article 20

The original of this Convention, of which the Chinese, English, French, Russian and Spanish texts are equally authentic, shall be deposited with the Secretary-General of the United Nations, who shall send certified copies thereof to all States.

IN WITNESS WHEREOF the undersigned, being duly authorized thereto by their respective Governments, have signed this Convention, opened for signature at New York on 14 December 1973.

5. International Convention against the Taking of Hostages

*Adopted by the General Assembly of the United Nations on
17 December 1979
In force on 3 June 1983
United Nations, Treaty Series, vol. 1316, No. 21931
Depositary: Secretary-General of the United Nations*

The States Parties to this Convention,

HAVING IN MIND the purposes and principles of the Charter of the United Nations concerning the maintenance of international peace and security and the promotion of friendly relations and co-operation among States,

RECOGNIZING in particular that everyone has the right to life, liberty and security of person, as set out in the Universal Declaration of Human Rights and the International Covenant on Civil and Political Rights,

REAFFIRMING the principle of equal rights and self-determination of peoples as enshrined in the Charter of the United Nations and the Declaration on Principles of International Law concerning Friendly Relations and Co-operation among States in accordance with the Charter of the United Nations, as well as in other relevant resolutions of the General Assembly,

CONSIDERING that the taking of hostages is an offence of grave concern to the international community and that, in accordance with the provisions of this Convention, any person committing an act of hostage taking shall either be prosecuted or extradited,

BEING CONVINCED that it is urgently necessary to develop international co-operation between States in devising and adopting effective measures for the prevention, prosecution and punishment of all acts of taking of hostages as manifestations of international terrorism,

Have agreed as follows:

Article 1

1. Any person who seizes or detains and threatens to kill, to injure or to continue to detain another person (hereinafter referred to as the "hostage") in order to compel a third party, namely, a State, an international intergovernmental organization, a natural or juridical person, or a group of persons, to do or abstain from doing any act as an explicit or implicit condition for the release of the hostage commits the offence of taking of hostages ("hostage-taking") within the meaning of this Convention.

2. Any person who:

(*a*)   attempts to commit an act of hostage-taking, or

(*b*)   participates as an accomplice of anyone who commits or attempts to commit an act of hostage-taking

likewise commits an offence for the purposes of this Convention.

Article 2

Each State Party shall make the offences set forth in Article 1 punishable by appropriate penalties which take into account the grave nature of those offences.

Article 3

1. The State Party in the territory of which the hostage is held by the offender shall take all measures it considers appropriate to ease the situation of the hostage, in particular, to secure his release and, after his release, to facilitate, when relevant, his departure.

2. If any object which the offender has obtained as a result of the taking of hostages comes into the custody of a State Party, that State Party shall return it as soon as possible to the hostage or the third party referred to in Article 1, as the case may be, or to the appropriate authorities thereof.

Article 4

States Parties shall co-operate in the prevention of the offences set forth in Article 1, particularly by:

(*a*)   taking all practicable measures to prevent preparations in their respective territories for the commission of those offences within or outside their territories, including measures to prohibit in their territories illegal activities of persons, groups and organizations that encourage, instigate, organize or engage in the perpetration of acts of taking of hostages;

(*b*)   exchanging information and co-ordinating the taking of administrative and other measures as appropriate to prevent the commission of those offences.

Article 5

1. Each State Party shall take such measures as may be necessary to establish its jurisdiction over any of the offences set forth in Article 1 which are committed:

(*a*)   in its territory or on board a ship or aircraft registered in that State;

(*b*)   by any of its nationals or, if that State considers it appropriate, by those stateless persons who have their habitual residence in its territory;

(*c*)   in order to compel that State to do or abstain from doing any act; or

(*d*)   with respect to a hostage who is a national of that State, if that State considers it appropriate.

2. Each State Party shall likewise take such measures as may be necessary to establish its jurisdiction over the offences set forth in Article 1 in cases where the alleged offender is present in its territory and it does not extradite him to any of the States mentioned in paragraph 1 of this Article.

3. This Convention does not exclude any criminal jurisdiction exercised in accordance with internal law.

Article 6

1. Upon being satisfied that the circumstances so warrant, any State Party in the territory of which the alleged offender is present shall, in accordance with its laws, take him into custody or take other measures to ensure his presence for such time as is necessary to enable any criminal or extradition proceedings to be instituted. That State Party shall immediately make a preliminary inquiry into the facts.

2. The custody or other measures referred to in paragraph 1 of this Article shall be notified without delay directly or through the Secretary-General of the United Nations to:

(*a*)   the State where the offence was committed;

(*b*)   the State against which compulsion has been directed or attempted;

(*c*)   the State of which the natural or juridical person against whom compulsion has been directed or attempted is a national;

(*d*)   the State of which the hostage is a national or in the territory of which he has his habitual residence;

(*e*)   the State of which the alleged offender is a national or, if he is a stateless person, in the territory of which he has his habitual residence;

(*f*)   the international intergovernmental organization against which compulsion has been directed or attempted;

(*g*)   all other States concerned.

3. Any person regarding whom the measures referred to in paragraph 1 of this Article are being taken shall be entitled:

(*a*)   to communicate without delay with the nearest appropriate representative of the State of which he is a national or which is otherwise entitled to establish such communication or, if he is a stateless person, the State in the territory of which he has his habitual residence;

(*b*)   to be visited by a representative of that State.

4. The rights referred to in paragraph 3 of this Article shall be exercised in conformity with the laws and regulations of the State in the territory of which the alleged offender is present subject to the proviso, however, that the said laws and regulations must enable full effect to be given to the purposes for which the rights accorded under paragraph 3 of this Article are intended.

5. The provisions of paragraphs 3 and 4 of this Article shall be without prejudice to the right of any State Party having a claim to jurisdiction in accordance with paragraph 1(*b*) of Article 5 to invite the International Committee of the Red Cross to communicate with and visit the alleged offender.

6. The State which makes the preliminary inquiry contemplated in paragraph 1 of this Article shall promptly report its findings to the States or organization referred to in paragraph 2 of this Article and indicate whether it intends to exercise jurisdiction.

Article 7

The State Party where the alleged offender is prosecuted shall in accordance with its laws communicate the final outcome of the proceedings to the Secretary-General of the United Nations, who shall transmit the information to the other States concerned and the international intergovernmental organizations concerned.

Article 8

1. The State Party in the territory of which the alleged offender is found shall, if it does not extradite him, be obliged, without exception whatsoever and whether or not the offence was committed in its territory, to submit the case to its competent authorities for the purpose of prosecution, through proceedings in accordance with the laws of that State. Those authorities shall take their decision in the same manner as in the

case of any ordinary offence of a grave nature under the law of that State.

2. Any person regarding whom proceedings are being carried out in connexion with any of the offences set forth in Article 1 shall be guaranteed fair treatment at all stages of the proceedings, including enjoyment of all the rights and guarantees provided by the law of the State in the territory of which he is present.

Article 9

1. A request for the extradition of an alleged offender, pursuant to this Convention, shall not be granted if the requested State Party has substantial grounds for believing:

(a)   that the request for extradition for an offence set forth in Article 1 has been made for the purpose of prosecuting or punishing a person on account of his race, religion, nationality, ethnic origin or political opinion; or

(b)   that the person's position may be prejudiced:

   (i)   for any of the reasons mentioned in subparagraph (a) of this paragraph, or

   (ii)   for the reason that communication with him by the appropriate authorities of the State entitled to exercise rights of protection cannot be effected.

2. With respect to the offences as defined in this Convention, the provisions of all extradition treaties and arrangements applicable between States Parties are modified as between States Parties to the extent that they are incompatible with this Convention.

Article 10

1. The offences set forth in Article 1 shall be deemed to be included as extraditable offences in any extradition treaty existing between States Parties. States Parties undertake to include such offences as extraditable offences in every extradition treaty to be concluded between them.

2. If a State Party which makes extradition conditional on the existence of a treaty receives a request for extradition from another State Party with which it has no extradition treaty, the requested State may at its option consider this Convention as the legal basis for extradition in respect of the offences set forth in Article 1. Extradition shall be subject to the other conditions provided by the law of the requested State.

3. States Parties which do not make extradition conditional on the existence of a treaty shall recognize the offences set forth in Article 1 as extraditable offences between themselves subject to the conditions provided by the law of the requested State.

4. The offences set forth in Article 1 shall be treated, for the purpose of extradition between States Parties, as if they had been committed not only in the place in which they occurred but also in the territories of the States required to establish their jurisdiction in accordance with paragraph 1 of Article 5.

Article 11

1. States Parties shall afford one another the greatest measure of assistance in connexion with criminal proceedings brought in respect of the offences set forth in Article 1, including the supply of all evidence at their disposal necessary for the proceedings.

2. The provisions of paragraph 1 of this Article shall not affect obligations concerning mutual judicial assistance embodied in any other treaty.

Article 12

In so far as the Geneva Conventions of 1949 for the protection of war victims or the Protocols Additional to those Conventions are applicable to a particular act of hostage-taking, and in so far as States Parties to this Convention are bound under those conventions to prosecute or hand over the hostage-taker, the present Convention shall not apply to an act of hostage-taking committed in the course of armed conflicts as defined in the Geneva Conventions of 1949 and the Protocols thereto, including armed conflicts mentioned in Article 1, paragraph 4, of Additional Protocol I of 1977, in which peoples are fighting against colonial domination and alien occupation and against racist regimes in the exercise of their right of self-determination, as enshrined in the Charter of the United Nations and the Declaration on Principles of International Law concerning Friendly Relations and Co-operation among States in accordance with the Charter of the United Nations.

Article 13

This Convention shall not apply where the offence is committed within a single State, the hostage and the alleged offender are nationals of that State and the alleged offender is found in the territory of that State.

Article 14

Nothing in this Convention shall be construed as justifying the violation of the territorial integrity or political independence of a State in contravention of the Charter of the United Nations.

Article 15

The provisions of this Convention shall not affect the application of the Treaties on Asylum, in force at the date of the adoption of this Convention, as between the States which are parties to those Treaties; but a State Party to this Convention may not invoke those Treaties with respect to another State Party to this Convention which is not a party to those treaties.

Article 16

1. Any dispute between two or more States Parties concerning the interpretation or application of this Convention which is not settled by negotiation shall, at the request of one of them, be submitted to arbitration. If within six months from the date of the request for arbitration the parties are unable to agree on the organization of the arbitration, any one of those parties may refer the dispute to the International Court of Justice by request in conformity with the Statute of the Court.

2. Each State may at the time of signature or ratification of this Convention or accession thereto declare that it does not consider itself bound by paragraph 1 of this Article. The other States Parties shall not be

bound by paragraph 1 of this Article with respect to any State Party which has made such a reservation.

3. Any State Party which has made a reservation in accordance with paragraph 2 of this Article may at any time withdraw that reservation by notification to the Secretary-General of the United Nations.

Article 17

1. This Convention is open for signature by all States until 31 December 1980 at United Nations Headquarters in New York.

2. This Convention is subject to ratification. The instruments of ratification shall be deposited with the Secretary-General of the United Nations.

3. This Convention is open for accession by any State. The instruments of accession shall be deposited with the Secretary-General of the United Nations.

Article 18

1. This Convention shall enter into force on the thirtieth day following the date of deposit of the twenty-second instrument of ratification or accession with the Secretary-General of the United Nations.

2. For each State ratifying or acceding to the Convention after the deposit of the twenty-second instrument of ratification or accession, the Convention shall enter into force on the thirtieth day after deposit by such State of its instrument of ratification or accession.

Article 19

1. Any State Party may denounce this Convention by written notification to the Secretary-General of the United Nations.

2. Denunciation shall take effect one year following the date on which notification is received by the Secretary-General of the United Nations.

Article 20

The original of this Convention, of which the Arabic, Chinese, English, French, Russian and Spanish texts are equally authentic, shall be deposited with the Secretary-General of the United Nations, who shall send certified copies thereof to all States.

IN WITNESS WHEREOF, the undersigned, being duly authorized thereto by their respective Governments, have signed this Convention, opened for signature at New York on 18 December 1979.

6. Convention on the Physical Protection of Nuclear Material

Adopted at Vienna on 26 October 1979
In force on 8 February 1987
United Nations, Treaty Series, vol. 1456, No. 24631
Depositary: Director General of the International Atomic Energy Agency

THE STATES PARTIES TO THIS CONVENTION,

RECOGNIZING the right of all States to develop and apply nuclear energy for peaceful purposes and their legitimate interests in the potential benefits to be derived from the peaceful application of nuclear energy,

CONVINCED of the need for facilitating international co-operation in the peaceful application of nuclear energy,

DESIRING to avert the potential dangers posed by the unlawful taking and use of nuclear material,

CONVINCED that offences relating to nuclear material are a matter of grave concern and that there is an urgent need to adopt appropriate and effective measures to ensure the prevention, detection and punishment of such offences,

AWARE OF THE NEED FOR international co-operation to establish, in conformity with the national law of each State Party and with this Convention, effective measures for the physical protection of nuclear material,

CONVINCED that this Convention should facilitate the safe transfer of nuclear material,

STRESSING also the importance of the physical protection of nuclear material in domestic use, storage and transport,

RECOGNIZING the importance of effective physical protection of nuclear material used for military purposes, and understanding that such material is and will continue to be accorded stringent physical protection,

Have agreed as follows:

Article 1

For the purposes of this Convention:

(*a*) "nuclear material" means plutonium except that with isotopic concentration exceeding 80% in plutonium-238; uranium-233; uranium enriched in the isotope 235 or 233; uranium containing the mixture of isotopes as occurring in nature other than in the form of ore or ore-residue; any material containing one or more of the foregoing;

(*b*) "uranium enriched in the isotope 235 or 233" means uranium containing the isotope 235 or 233 or both in an amount such that the abundance ratio of the sum of these isotopes to the isotope 238 is greater than the ratio of the isotope 235 to the isotope 238 occurring in nature;

(*c*) "international nuclear transport" means the carriage of a consignment of nuclear material by any means of transportation intended to go beyond the territory of the State where the shipment originates beginning with the departure from a facility of the shipper in that State and ending with the arrival at a facility of the receiver within the State of ultimate destination.

Article 2

1. This Convention shall apply to nuclear material used for peaceful purposes while in international nuclear transport.

2. With the exception of Articles 3 and 4 and paragraph 3 of Article 5, this Convention shall also apply to nuclear material used for peaceful purposes while in domestic use, storage and transport.

3. Apart from the commitments expressly undertaken by States Parties in the Articles covered by paragraph 2 with respect to nuclear material used for peaceful purposes while in domestic use, storage and transport, nothing in this Convention shall be interpreted as affecting the

sovereign rights of a State regarding the domestic use, storage and transport of such nuclear material.

Article 3

Each State Party shall take appropriate steps within the framework of its national law and consistent with international law to ensure as far as practicable that, during international nuclear transport, nuclear material within its territory, or on board a ship or aircraft under its jurisdiction insofar as such ship or aircraft is engaged in the transport to or from that State, is protected at the levels described in Annex I.

Article 4

1. Each State Party shall not export or authorize the export of nuclear material unless the State Party has received assurances that such material will be protected during the international nuclear transport at the levels described in Annex I.

2. Each State Party shall not import or authorize the import of nuclear material from a State not party to this Convention unless the State Party has received assurances that such material will during the international nuclear transport be protected at the levels described in Annex I.

3. A State Party shall not allow the transit of its territory by land or internal waterways or through its airports or seaports of nuclear material between States that are not parties to this Convention unless the State Party has received assurances as far as practicable that this nuclear material will be protected during international nuclear transport at the levels described in Annex I.

4. Each State Party shall apply within the framework of its national law the levels of physical protection described in Annex I to nuclear material being transported from a part of that State to another part of the same State through international waters or airspace.

5. The State Party responsible for receiving assurances that the nuclear material will be protected at the levels described in Annex I according to paragraphs 1 to 3 shall identify and inform in advance States

which the nuclear material is expected to transit by land or internal waterways, or whose airports or seaports it is expected to enter.

6. The responsibility for obtaining assurances referred to in paragraph 1 may be transferred, by mutual agreement, to the State Party involved in the transport as the importing State.

7. Nothing in this Article shall be interpreted as in any way affecting the territorial sovereignty and jurisdiction of a State, including that over its airspace and territorial sea.

Article 5

1. States Parties shall identify and make known to each other directly or through the International Atomic Energy Agency their central authority and point of contact having responsibility for physical protection of nuclear material and for co-ordinating recovery and response operations in the event of any unauthorized removal, use or alteration of nuclear material or in the event of credible threat thereof.

2. In the case of theft, robbery or any other unlawful taking of nuclear material or of credible threat thereof, States Parties shall, in accordance with their national law, provide co-operation and assistance to the maximum feasible extent in the recovery and protection of such material to any State that so requests. In particular:

(a)   a State Party shall take appropriate steps to inform as soon as possible other States, which appear to it to be concerned, of any theft, robbery or other unlawful taking of nuclear material or credible threat thereof and to inform, where appropriate, international organizations;

(b)   as appropriate, the States Parties concerned shall exchange information with each other or international organizations with a view to protecting threatened nuclear material, verifying the integrity of the shipping container, or recovering unlawfully taken nuclear material and shall:

(i)   co-ordinate their efforts through diplomatic and other agreed channels;

(ii)   render assistance, if requested;

(iii)   ensure the return of nuclear material stolen or missing as a consequence of the above-mentioned events.

The means of implementation of this co-operation shall be determined by the States Parties concerned.

3. States Parties shall co-operate and consult as appropriate, with each other directly or through international organizations, with a view to obtaining guidance on the design, maintenance and improvement of systems of physical protection of nuclear material in international transport.

Article 6

1. States Parties shall take appropriate measures consistent with their national law to protect the confidentiality of any information which they receive in confidence by virtue of the provisions of this Convention from another State Party or through participation in an activity carried out for the implementation of this Convention. If States Parties provide information to international organizations in confidence, steps shall be taken to ensure that the confidentiality of such information is protected.

2. States Parties shall not be required by this Convention to provide any information which they are not permitted to communicate pursuant to national law or which would jeopardize the security of the State concerned or the physical protection of nuclear material.

Article 7

1. The intentional commission of:

(*a*)   an act without lawful authority which constitutes the receipt, possession, use, transfer, alteration, disposal or dispersal of nuclear material and which causes or is likely to cause death or serious injury to any person or substantial damage to property;

(*b*)   a theft or robbery of nuclear material;

(*c*)   an embezzlement or fraudulent obtaining of nuclear material;

(*d*)   an act constituting a demand for nuclear material by threat or use of force or by any other form of intimidation;

(*e*)   a threat:

    (i)   to use nuclear material to cause death or serious injury to any person or substantial property damage, or

    (ii)   to commit an offence described in sub-paragraph (*b*) in order to compel a natural or legal person, international organization or State to do or to refrain from doing any act;

(*f*)   an attempt to commit any offence described in paragraphs (*a*), (*b*) or (*c*); and

(*g*)   an act which constitutes participation in any offence described in paragraphs (*a*) to (*f*)

shall be made a punishable offence by each State Party under its national law.

2. Each State Party shall make the offences described in this Article punishable by appropriate penalties which take into account their grave nature.

Article 8

1. Each State Party shall take such measures as may be necessary to establish its jurisdiction over the offences set forth in Article 7 in the following cases:

(*a*)   when the offence is committed in the territory of that State or on board a ship or aircraft registered in that State;

(*b*)   when the alleged offender is a national of that State.

2.   Each State Party shall likewise take such measures as may be necessary to establish its jurisdiction over these offences in cases where

the alleged offender is presented in its territory and it does not extradite him pursuant to Article 11 to any of the States mentioned in paragraph 1.

3.   This Convention does not exclude any criminal jurisdiction exercised in accordance with national law.

4.   In addition to the States Parties mentioned in paragraphs 1 and 2, each State Party may, consistent with international law, establish its jurisdiction over the offences set forth in Article 7 when it is involved in international nuclear transport as the exporting or importing State.

Article 9

Upon being satisfied that the circumstances so warrant, the State Party in whose territory the alleged offender is present shall take appropriate measures, including detention, under its national law to ensure his presence for the purpose of prosecution or extradition. Measures taken according to this Article shall be notified without delay to the States required to establish jurisdiction pursuant to Article 8 and, where appropriate, all other States concerned.

Article 10

The State Party in whose territory the alleged offender is present shall, if it does not extradite him, submit, without exception whatsoever and without undue delay, the case to its competent authorities for the purpose of prosecution, through proceedings in accordance with the laws of that State.

Article 11

1. The offences in Article 7 shall be deemed to be included as extraditable offences in any extradition treaty existing between States Parties. States Parties undertake to include those offences as extraditable offences in every future extradition treaty to be concluded between them.

2. If a State Party which makes extradition conditional on the existence of a treaty receives a request for extradition from another State Party with which it has no extradition treaty, it may at its option consider this Convention as the legal basis for extradition in respect of those

offences. Extradition shall be subject to the other conditions provided by the law of the requested State.

3. States Parties which do not make extradition conditional on the existence of a treaty shall recognize those offences as extraditable offences between themselves subject to the conditions provided by the law of the requested State.

4. Each of the offences shall be treated, for the purpose of extradition between States Parties, as if it had been committed not only in the place in which it occurred but also in the territories of the States Parties required to establish their jurisdiction in accordance with paragraph 1 of Article 8.

Article 12

Any person regarding whom proceedings are being carried out in connection with any of the offences set forth in Article 7 shall be guaranteed fair treatment at all stages of the proceedings.

Article 13

1. States Parties shall afford one another the greatest measure of assistance in connection with criminal proceedings brought in respect of the offences set forth in Article 7, including the supply of evidence at their disposal necessary for the proceedings. The law of the State requested shall apply in all cases.

2. The provisions of paragraph 1 shall not affect obligations under any other treaty, bilateral or multilateral, which governs or will govern, in whole or in part, mutual assistance in criminal matters.

Article 14

1. Each State Party shall inform the depositary of its laws and regulations which give effect to this Convention. The depositary shall communicate such information periodically to all States Parties.

2. The State Party where an alleged offender is prosecuted shall, wherever practicable, first communicate the final outcome of the

proceedings to the States directly concerned. The State Party shall also communicate the final outcome to the depositary who shall inform all States.

3. Where an offence involves nuclear material used for peaceful purposes in domestic use, storage or transport, and both the alleged offender and the nuclear material remain in the territory of the State Party in which the offence was committed, nothing in this Convention shall be interpreted as requiring that State Party to provide information concerning criminal proceedings arising out of such an offence.

Article 15

The Annexes constitute an integral part of this Convention.

Article 16

1. A conference of States Parties shall be convened by the depositary five years after the entry into force of this Convention to review the implementation of the Convention and its adequacy as concerns the preamble, the whole of the operative part and the annexes in the light of the then prevailing situation.

2. At intervals of not less than five years thereafter, the majority of States Parties may obtain, by submitting a proposal to this effect to the depositary, the convening of further conferences with the same objective.

Article 17

1. In the event of a dispute between two or more States Parties concerning the interpretation or application of this Convention, such States Parties shall consult with a view to the settlement of the dispute by negotiation, or by any other peaceful means of settling disputes acceptable to all parties to the dispute.

2. Any dispute of this character which cannot be settled in the manner prescribed in paragraph 1 shall, at the request of any party to such dispute, be submitted to arbitration or referred to the International Court of Justice for decision. Where a dispute is submitted to arbitration, if, within six months from the date of the request, the parties to the dispute

are unable to agree on the organization of the arbitration, a party may request the President of the International Court of Justice or the Secretary-General of the United Nations to appoint one or more arbitrators. In case of conflicting requests by the parties to the dispute, the request to the Secretary-General of the United Nations shall have priority.

3. Each State Party may at the time of signature, ratification, acceptance or approval of this Convention or accession thereto declare that it does not consider itself bound by either or both of the dispute settlement procedures provided for in paragraph 2. The other States Parties shall not be bound by a dispute settlement procedure provided for in paragraph 2, with respect to a State Party which has made a reservation to that procedure.

4. Any State Party which has made a reservation in accordance with paragraph 3 may at any time withdraw that reservation by notification to the depositary.

Article 18

1. This Convention shall be open for signature by all States at the Headquarters of the International Atomic Energy Agency in Vienna and at the Headquarters of the United Nations in New York from 3 March 1980 until its entry into force.

2. This Convention is subject to ratification, acceptance or approval by the signatory States.

3. After its entry into force, this Convention will be open for accession by all States.

4. (*a*) This Convention shall be open for signature or accession by international organizations and regional organizations of an integration or other nature, provided that any such organization is constituted by sovereign States and has competence in respect of the negotiation, conclusion and application of international agreements in matters covered by this Convention.

(*b*) In matters within their competence, such organizations shall, on their own behalf, exercise the rights and fulfil the responsibilities which this Convention attributes to States Parties.

(*c*) When becoming party to this Convention such an organization shall communicate to the depository a declaration indicating which States are members thereof and which Articles of this Convention do not apply to it.

(*d*) Such an organization shall not hold any vote additional to those of its Member States.

5. Instruments of ratification, acceptance, approval or accession shall be deposited with depositary.

Article 19

1. This Convention shall enter into force on the thirtieth day following the date of deposit of the twenty-first instrument of ratification, acceptance or approval with the depositary.

2. For each State ratifying, accepting, approving or acceding to the Convention after the date of deposit of the twenty-first instrument of ratification, acceptance or approval, the Convention shall enter into force on the thirtieth day after the deposit by such State of its instrument of ratification, acceptance, approval or accession.

Article 20

1. Without prejudice to Article 16 a State Party may propose amendments to this Convention. The proposed amendment shall be submitted to the depositary who shall circulate it immediately to all States Parties. If a majority of States Parties request the depositary to convene a conference to consider the proposed amendments, the depositary shall invite all States Parties to attend such a conference to begin not sooner than thirty days after the invitations are issued. Any amendment adopted at the conference by a two-thirds majority of all States Parties shall be promptly circulated by the depositary to all States Parties.

2. The amendment shall enter into force for each State Party that deposits its instrument of ratification, acceptance or approval of the amendment on the thirtieth day after the date on which two thirds of the

States Parties have deposited their instruments of ratification, acceptance or approval with the depositary. Thereafter, the amendment shall enter into force for any other State Party on the day on which that State Party deposits its instrument of ratification, acceptance or approval of the amendment.

Article 21

1. Any State Party may denounce this Convention by written notification to the depositary.

2. Denunciation shall take effect one hundred and eighty days following the date on which notification is received by the depositary.

Article 22

The depositary shall promptly notify all States of:

(*a*)   each signature of this Convention;

(*b*)   each deposit of an instrument of ratification, acceptance, approval or accession;

(*c*)   any reservation or withdrawal in accordance with Article 17;

(*d*)   any communication made by an organization in accordance with paragraph 4(*c*) of Article 18;

(*e*)   the entry into force of this Convention;

(*f*)   the entry into force of any amendment to this Convention; and

(*g*)   any denunciation made under Article 21.

Article 23

The original of this Convention, of which the Arabic, Chinese, English, French, Russian and Spanish texts are equally authentic, shall be deposited with the Director General of the International Atomic Energy Agency who shall send certified copies thereof to all States.

IN WITNESS WHEREOF, the undersigned, being duly authorized, have signed this Convention, opened for signature at Vienna and at New York on 3 March 1980.

ANNEX I

LEVELS OF PHYSICAL PROTECTION TO BE APPLIED IN INTERNATIONAL TRANSPORT OF NUCLEAR MATERIALS AS CATEGORIZED IN ANNEX II

1. Levels of physical protection for nuclear material during storage incidental to international nuclear transport include:

(*a*)   For Category III materials, storage within an area to which access is controlled;

(*b*)   For Category II materials, storage within an area under constant surveillance by guards or electronic devices, surrounded by a physical barrier with a limited number of points of entry under appropriate control or any area with an equivalent level of physical protection;

(*c*)   For Category I material, storage within a protected area as defined for Category II above, to which, in addition, access is restricted to persons whose trustworthiness has been determined, and which is under surveillance by guards who are in close communication with appropriate response forces. Specific measures taken in this context should have as their object the detection and prevention of any assault, unauthorized access or unauthorized removal of material.

2. Levels of physical protection for nuclear material during international transport include:

(*a*)   For Category II and III materials, transportation shall take place under special precautions including prior arrangements among sender, receiver, and carrier, and prior agreement between natural or legal persons subject to the jurisdiction and regulation of exporting and importing States, specifying time, place and procedures for transferring transport responsibility;

(*b*)   For Category I materials, transportation shall take place under special precautions identified above for transportation of Category II and III materials, and in addition, under constant surveillance by escorts and under conditions which assure close communication with appropriate response forces;

(c) For natural uranium other than in the form of ore or ore-residue, transportation protection for quantities exceeding 500 kilograms uranium shall include advance notification of shipment specifying mode of transport, expected time of arrival and confirmation of receipt of shipment.

ANNEX II

TABLE: CATEGORIZATION OF NUCLEAR MATERIAL

Material	Form	Category I	II	IIIᶜ
1. Plutoniumᵃ	Unirradiatedᵇ	2 kg or more	Less than 2 kg but more than 500 g	500 g or less but more than 15 g
2. Uranium-235	Unirradiatedᵇ -uranium enriched to 20% ^{235}U or more	5 kg or more	Less than 5 kg but more than 1 kg	1 kg or less but more than 15 g
	-uranium enriched to 10% ^{235}U but less than 20%		10 kg or more	Less than 10 kg but more than 1 kg
	-uranium enriched above natural, but less than 10% ^{235}U			10 kg or more

3. Uranium-233	Unirradiated[b]	2 kg or more	Less than 2 kg but more than 500 g	500 g or less but more than 15 g
4. Irradiated fuel			Depleted or natural uranium, thorium or low-enriched fuel (less than 10% fissile content)[d,e]	

[a] All plutonium except that with isotopic concentration exceeding 80% in plutonium-238.

[b] Material not irradiated in a reactor or material irradiated in a reactor but with a radiation level equal to or less than 100 rads/hour at one metre unshielded.

[c] Quantities not falling in Category III and natural uranium should be protected in accordance with prudent management practice.

[d] Although this level of protection is recommended, it would be open to States, upon evaluation of the specific circumstances, to assign a different category of physical protection.

[e] Other fuel which by virtue of its original fissile material content is classified as Category I and II before irradiation may be reduced one category level while the radiation level from the fuel exceeds 100 rads/hour at one metre unshielded.

7. Protocol for the Suppression of Unlawful Acts of Violence at Airports Serving International Civil Aviation, supplementary to the Convention for the Suppression of Unlawful Acts against the Safety of Civil Aviation, done at Montreal on 23 September 1971

Done at Montreal on 24 February 1988
In force on 6 August 1989
ICAO Doc. 9518
Depositary: Russian Federation, United Kingdom of Great Britain and Northern Ireland, the United States of America and the International Civil Aviation Organization

THE STATES PARTIES TO THIS PROTOCOL

CONSIDERING that unlawful acts of violence which endanger or are likely to endanger the safety of persons at airports serving international civil aviation or which jeopardize the safe operation of such airports undermine the confidence of the peoples of the world in safety at such airports and disturb the safe and orderly conduct of civil aviation for all States;

CONSIDERING that the occurrence of such acts is a matter of grave concern to the international community and that, for the purpose of deterring such acts, there is an urgent need to provide appropriate measures for punishment of offenders;

CONSIDERING that it is necessary to adopt provisions supplementary to those of the Convention for the Suppression of Unlawful Acts against the Safety of Civil Aviation, done at Montreal on 23 September 1971, to deal with such unlawful acts of violence at airports serving international civil aviation;

Have agreed as follows:

Article I

This Protocol supplements the Convention for the Suppression of Unlawful Acts against the Safety of Civil Aviation, done at Montreal on 23 September 1971 (hereinafter referred to as "the Convention"), and, as between the Parties to this Protocol, the Convention and the Protocol shall be read and interpreted together as one single instrument.

Article II

1. In Article 1 of the Convention, the following shall be added as new paragraph 1 *bis*:

"1 *bis*. Any person commits an offence if he unlawfully and intentionally, using any device, substance or weapon:

(*a*)   performs an act of violence against a person at an airport serving international civil aviation which causes or is likely to cause serious injury or death; or

(*b*)   destroys or seriously damages the facilities of an airport serving international civil aviation or aircraft not in service located thereon or disrupts the services of the airport,

if such an act endangers or is likely to endanger safety at that airport."

2. In paragraph 2(*a*) of Article 1 of the Convention, the following words shall be inserted after the words "paragraph 1":

"or paragraph 1 *bis*".

Article III

In Article 5 of the Convention, the following shall be added as paragraph 2 *bis*:

"2 *bis*. Each Contracting State shall likewise take such measures as may be necessary to establish its jurisdiction over the offences mentioned in Article 1, paragraph 1 *bis*, and in Article 1, paragraph

2, in so far as that paragraph relates to those offences, in the case where the alleged offender is present in its territory and it does not extradite him pursuant to Article 8 to the State mentioned in paragraph 1(*a*) of this Article."

Article IV

This Protocol shall be open for signature at Montreal on 24 February 1988 by States participating in the International Conference on Air Law held at Montreal from 9 to 24 February 1988. After 1 March 1988, the Protocol shall be open for signature to all States in London, Moscow, Washington and Montreal, until it enters into force in accordance with Article VI.

Article V

1. This Protocol shall be subject to ratification by the signatory States.

2. Any State which is not a Contracting State to the Convention may ratify this Protocol if at the same time it ratifies or accedes to the Convention in accordance with Article 15 thereof.

3. Instruments of ratification shall be deposited with the Governments of the Union of Soviet Socialist Republics, the United Kingdom of Great Britain and Northern Ireland and the United States of America or with the International Civil Aviation Organization, which are hereby designated the Depositaries.

Article VI

1. As soon as ten of the signatory States have deposited their instruments of ratification of this Protocol, it shall enter into force between them on the thirtieth day after the date of the deposit of the tenth instrument of ratification. It shall enter into force for each State which deposits its instrument of ratification after that date on the thirtieth day after deposit of its instrument of ratification.

2. As soon as this Protocol enters into force, it shall be registered by the Depositaries pursuant to Article 102 of the Charter of the United

Nations and pursuant to Article 83 of the Convention on International Civil Aviation (Chicago, 1944).

Article VII

1. This Protocol shall, after it has entered into force, be open for accession by any non-signatory State.

2. Any State which is not a Contracting State to the Convention may accede to this Protocol if at the same time it ratifies or accedes to the Convention in accordance with Article 15 thereof.

3. Instruments of accession shall be deposited with the Depositaries and accession shall take effect on the thirtieth day after the deposit.

Article VIII

1. Any Party to this Protocol may denounce it by written notification addressed to the Depositaries.

2. Denunciation shall take effect six months following the date on which notification is received by the Depositaries.

3. Denunciation of this Protocol shall not of itself have the effect of denunciation of the Convention.

4. Denunciation of the Convention by a Contracting State to the Convention as supplemented by this Protocol shall also have the effect of denunciation of this Protocol.

Article IX

1. The Depositaries shall promptly inform all signatory and acceding States to this Protocol and all signatory and acceding States to the Convention:

(*a*)   of the date of each signature and the date of deposit of each instrument of ratification of, or accession to, this Protocol, and

(*b*)   of the receipt of any notification of denunciation of this Protocol and the date thereof.

2. The Depositaries shall also notify the States referred to in paragraph 1 of the date on which this Protocol enters into force in accordance with Article VI.

IN WITNESS WHEREOF the undersigned Plenipotentiaries, being duly authorized thereto by their Governments, have signed this Protocol.

DONE at Montreal on the twenty-fourth day of February of the year One Thousand Nine Hundred and Eighty-eight, in four originals, each being drawn up in four authentic texts in the English, French, Russian and Spanish languages.

---

8. Convention for the Suppression of Unlawful Acts against the Safety of Maritime Navigation

Done at Rome on 10 March 1988
In force on 1 March 1992
IMO Doc. SUA/CONF/15/Rev.1
Depositary: Secretary-General of the International Maritime
Organization

THE STATES PARTIES TO THIS CONVENTION,

HAVING IN MIND the purposes and principles of the Charter of the United Nations concerning the maintenance of international peace and security and the promotion of friendly relations and co-operation among States,

RECOGNIZING in particular that everyone has the right to life, liberty and security of person, as set out in the Universal Declaration of Human Rights and the International Covenant on Civil and Political Rights,

DEEPLY CONCERNED about the world-wide escalation of acts of terrorism in all its forms, which endanger or take innocent human lives, jeopardize fundamental freedoms and seriously impair the dignity of human beings,

CONSIDERING that unlawful acts against the safety of maritime navigation jeopardize the safety of persons and property, seriously affect the operation of maritime services, and undermine the confidence of the peoples of the world in the safety of maritime navigation,

CONSIDERING that the occurrence of such acts is a matter of grave concern to the international community as a whole,

BEING CONVINCED of the urgent need to develop international co-operation between States in devising and adopting effective and practical measures for the prevention of all unlawful acts against the safety of maritime navigation, and the prosecution and punishment of their perpetrators,

RECALLING resolution 40/61 of the General Assembly of the United Nations of 9 December 1985 which, *inter alia*, "urges all States, unilaterally and in co-operation with other States, as well as relevant United Nations organs, to contribute to the progressive elimination of causes underlying international terrorism and to pay special attention to all situations, including colonialism, racism and situations involving mass and flagrant violations of human rights and fundamental freedoms and those involving alien occupation, that may give rise to international terrorism and may endanger international peace and security",

RECALLING FURTHER that resolution 40/61 "unequivocally condemns, as criminal, all acts, methods and practices of terrorism wherever and by whomever committed, including those which jeopardize friendly relations among States and their security",

RECALLING ALSO that by resolution 40/61, the International Maritime Organization was invited to "study the problem of terrorism aboard or against ships with a view to making recommendations on appropriate measures",

HAVING IN MIND resolution A.584(14) of 20 November 1985, of the Assembly of the International Maritime Organization, which called for development of measures to prevent unlawful acts which threaten the safety of ships and the security of their passengers and crews,

NOTING that acts of the crew which are subject to normal shipboard discipline are outside the purview of this Convention,

AFFIRMING the desirability of monitoring rules and standards relating to the prevention and control of unlawful acts against ships and persons on board ships, with a view to updating them as necessary, and, to this effect, taking note with satisfaction of the Measures to Prevent Unlawful Acts against Passengers and Crews on Board Ships, recommended by the Maritime Safety Committee of the International Maritime Organization,

AFFIRMING FURTHER that matters not regulated by this Convention continue to be governed by the rules and principles of general international law,

RECOGNIZING the need for all States, in combating unlawful acts against the safety of maritime navigation, strictly to comply with rules and principles of general international law,

Have agreed as follows:

Article 1

For the purposes of this Convention, "ship" means a vessel of any type whatsoever not permanently attached to the sea-bed, including dynamically supported craft, submersibles, or any other floating craft.

Article 2

1. This Convention does not apply to:

(*a*)   a warship; or

(*b*)   a ship owned or operated by a State when being used as a naval auxiliary or for customs or police purposes; or

(*c*)   a ship which has been withdrawn from navigation or laid up.

2. Nothing in this Convention affects the immunities of warships and other government ships operated for non-commercial purposes.

Article 3

1. Any person commits an offence if that person unlawfully and intentionally:

(*a*)   seizes or exercises control over a ship by force or threat thereof or any other form of intimidation; or

(*b*)   performs an act of violence against a person on board a ship if that act is likely to endanger the safe navigation of that ship; or

(*c*)   destroys a ship or causes damage to a ship or to its cargo which is likely to endanger the safe navigation of that ship; or (*d*)   places or causes to be placed on a ship, by any means whatsoever, a device or substance which is likely to destroy that ship, or cause damage to that ship or its cargo which endangers or is likely to endanger the safe navigation of that ship; or

(*e*)   destroys or seriously damages maritime navigational facilities or seriously interferes with their operation, if any such act is likely to endanger the safe navigation of a ship; or

(*f*)   communicates information which he knows to be false, thereby endangering the safe navigation of a ship; or

(*g*)   injures or kills any person, in connection with the commission or the attempted commission of any of the offences set forth in subparagraphs (*a*) to (*f*).

2. Any person also commits an offence if that person:

(*a*)   attempts to commit any of the offences set forth in paragraph 1; or

(*b*)   abets the commission of any of the offences set forth in paragraph 1 perpetrated by any person or is otherwise an accomplice of a person who commits such an offence; or

(*c*)   threatens, with or without a condition, as is provided for under national law, aimed at compelling a physical or juridical person to do or refrain from doing any act, to commit any of the offences set forth in paragraph 1, subparagraphs (*b*), (*c*) and (*e*), if that threat is likely to endanger the safe navigation of the ship in question.

Article 4

1. This Convention applies if the ship is navigating or is scheduled to navigate into, through or from waters beyond the outer limit of the territorial sea of a single State, or the lateral limits of its territorial sea with adjacent States.

2. In cases where the Convention does not apply pursuant to paragraph 1, it nevertheless applies when the offender or the alleged offender is found in the territory of a State Party other than the State

referred to in paragraph 1.

Article 5

Each State Party shall make the offences set forth in Article 3 punishable by appropriate penalties which take into account the grave nature of those offences.

Article 6

1. Each State Party shall take such measures as may be necessary to establish its jurisdiction over the offences set forth in Article 3 when the offence is committed:

(*a*)   against or on board a ship flying the flag of the State at the time the offence is committed; or

(*b*)   in the territory of that State, including its territorial sea; or

(*c*)   by a national of that State.

2. A State Party may also establish its jurisdiction over any such offence when:

(*a*)   it is committed by a stateless person whose habitual residence is in that State; or

(*b*)   during its commission a national of that State is seized, threatened, injured or killed; or

(*c*)   it is committed in an attempt to compel that State to do or abstain from doing any act.

3. Any State Party which has established jurisdiction mentioned in paragraph 2 shall notify the Secretary-General of the International Maritime Organization (hereinafter referred to as "the Secretary-General"). If such State Party subsequently rescinds that jurisdiction, it shall notify the Secretary-General.

4. Each State Party shall take such measures as may be necessary

to establish its jurisdiction over the offences set forth in Article 3 in cases where the alleged offender is present in its territory and it does not extradite him to any of the States Parties which have established their jurisdiction in accordance with paragraphs 1 and 2 of this Article.

5. This Convention does not exclude any criminal jurisdiction exercised in accordance with national law.

Article 7

1. Upon being satisfied that the circumstances so warrant, any State Party in the territory of which the offender or the alleged offender is present shall, in accordance with its law, take him into custody or take other measures to ensure his presence for such time as is necessary to enable any criminal or extradition proceeding to be instituted.

2. Such State shall immediately make a preliminary inquiry into the facts, in accordance with its own legislation.

3. Any person regarding whom the measures referred to in paragraph 1 are being taken shall be entitled to:

(*a*) communicate without delay with the nearest appropriate representative of the State of which he is a national or which is otherwise entitled to establish such communication or, if he is a stateless person, the State in the territory of which he has his habitual residence;

(*b*) be visited by a representative of that State.

4. The rights referred to in paragraph 3 shall be exercised in conformity with the laws and regulations of the State in the territory of which the offender or the alleged offender is present, subject to the proviso that the said laws and regulations must enable full effect to be given to the purposes for which the rights accorded under paragraph 3 are intended.

5. When a State Party, pursuant to this Article, has taken a person into custody, it shall immediately notify the States which have established jurisdiction in accordance with Article 6, paragraph 1 and, if it considers

it advisable, any other interested States, of the fact that such person is in custody and of the circumstances which warrant his detention. The State which makes the preliminary inquiry contemplated in paragraph 2 of this Article shall promptly report its findings to the said States and shall indicate whether it intends to exercise jurisdiction.

Article 8

1. The master of a ship of a State Party (the "flag State") may deliver to the authorities of any other State Party (the "receiving State") any person who he has reasonable grounds to believe has committed one of the offences set forth in Article 3.

2. The flag State shall ensure that the master of its ship is obliged, whenever practicable, and if possible before entering the territorial sea of the receiving State carrying on board any person whom the master intends to deliver in accordance with paragraph 1, to give notification to the authorities of the receiving State of his intention to deliver such person and the reasons therefor.

3. The receiving State shall accept the delivery, except where it has grounds to consider that the Convention is not applicable to the acts giving rise to the delivery, and shall proceed in accordance with the provisions of Article 7. Any refusal to accept a delivery shall be accompanied by a statement of the reasons for refusal.

4. The flag State shall ensure that the master of its ship is obliged to furnish the authorities of the receiving State with the evidence in the master's possession which pertains to the alleged offence.

5. A receiving State which has accepted the delivery of a person in accordance with paragraph 3 may, in turn, request the flag State to accept delivery of that person. The flag State shall consider any such request, and if it accedes to the request it shall proceed in accordance with Article 7. If the flag State declines a request, it shall furnish the receiving State with a statement of the reasons therefor.

Article 9

Nothing in this Convention shall affect in any way the rules of international law pertaining to the competence of States to exercise investigative or enforcement jurisdiction on board ships not flying their flag.

Article 10

1. The State Party in the territory of which the offender or the alleged offender is found shall, in cases to which Article 6 applies, if it does not extradite him, be obliged, without exception whatsoever and whether or not the offence was committed in its territory, to submit the case without delay to its competent authorities for the purpose of prosecution, through proceedings in accordance with the laws of that State. Those authorities shall take their decision in the same manner as in the case of any other offence of a grave nature under the law of that State.

2. Any person regarding whom proceedings are being carried out in connection with any of the offences set forth in Article 3 shall be guaranteed fair treatment at all stages of the proceedings, including enjoyment of all the rights and guarantees provided for such proceedings by the law of the State in the territory of which he is present.

Article 11

1. The offences set forth in Article 3 shall be deemed to be included as extraditable offences in any extradition treaty existing between any of the States Parties. States Parties undertake to include such offences as extraditable offences in every extradition treaty to be concluded between them.

2. If a State Party which makes extradition conditional on the existence of a treaty receives a request for extradition from another State Party with which it has no extradition treaty, the requested State Party may, at its option, consider this Convention as a legal basis for extradition in respect of the offences set forth in Article 3. Extradition shall be subject to the other conditions provided by the law of the requested State Party.

3. States Parties which do not make extradition conditional on the existence of a treaty shall recognize the offences set forth in Article 3 as extraditable offences between themselves, subject to the conditions provided by the law of the requested State.

4. If necessary, the offences set forth in Article 3 shall be treated, for the purposes of extradition between States Parties, as if they had been committed not only in the place in which they occurred but also in a place within the jurisdiction of the State Party requesting extradition.

5. A State Party which receives more than one request for extradition from States which have established jurisdiction in accordance with Article 6 and which decides not to prosecute shall, in selecting the State to which the offender or alleged offender is to be extradited, pay due regard to the interests and responsibilities of the State Party whose flag the ship was flying at the time of the commission of the offence.

6. In considering a request for the extradition of an alleged offender pursuant to this Convention, the requested State shall pay due regard to whether his rights as set forth in Article 7, paragraph 3, can be effected in the requesting State.

7. With respect to the offences as defined in this Convention, the provisions of all extradition treaties and arrangements applicable between States Parties are modified as between States Parties to the extent that they are incompatible with this Convention.

Article 12

1. State Parties shall afford one another the greatest measure of assistance in connection with criminal proceedings brought in respect of the offences set forth in Article 3, including assistance in obtaining evidence at their disposal necessary for the proceedings.

2. States Parties shall carry out their obligations under paragraph 1 in conformity with any treaties on mutual assistance that may exist between them. In the absence of such treaties, States Parties shall afford each other assistance in accordance with their national law.

Article 13

1. States Parties shall co-operate in the prevention of the offences set forth in Article 3, particularly by:

(*a*)   taking all practicable measures to prevent preparations in their respective territories for the commission of those offences within or outside their territories;

(*b*)   exchanging information in accordance with their national law, and co-ordinating administrative and other measures taken as appropriate to prevent the commission of offences set forth in Article 3.

2. When, due to the commission of an offence set forth in Article 3, the passage of a ship has been delayed or interrupted, any State Party in whose territory the ship or passengers or crew are present shall be bound to exercise all possible efforts to avoid a ship, its passengers, crew or cargo being unduly detained or delayed.

Article 14

Any State Party having reason to believe that an offence set forth in Article 3 will be committed shall, in accordance with its national law, furnish as promptly as possible any relevant information in its possession to those States which it believes would be the States having established jurisdiction in accordance with Article 6.

Article 15

1. Each State Party shall, in accordance with its national law, provide to the Secretary-General, as promptly as possible, any relevant information in its possession concerning:

(*a*)   the circumstances of the offence;

(*b*)   the action taken pursuant to Article 13, paragraph 2;

(*c*)   the measures taken in relation to the offender or the alleged offender and, in particular, the results of any extradition proceedings or other legal proceedings.

2. The State Party where the alleged offender is prosecuted shall, in accordance with its national law, communicate the final outcome of the proceedings to the Secretary-General.

3. The information transmitted in accordance with paragraphs 1 and 2 shall be communicated by the Secretary-General to all States Parties, to Members of the International Maritime Organization (hereinafter referred to as "the Organization"), to the other States concerned, and to the appropriate international intergovernmental organizations.

Article 16

1. Any dispute between two or more States Parties concerning the interpretation or application of this Convention which cannot be settled through negotiation within a reasonable time shall, at the request of one of them, be submitted to arbitration. If, within six months from the date of the request for arbitration, the parties are unable to agree on the organization of the arbitration any one of those parties may refer the dispute to the International Court of Justice by request in conformity with the Statute of the Court.

2. Each State may at the time of signature or ratification, acceptance or approval of this Convention or accession thereto, declare that it does not consider itself bound by any or all of the provisions of paragraph 1. The other States Parties shall not be bound by those provisions with respect to any State Party which has made such a reservation.

3. Any State which has made a reservation in accordance with paragraph 2 may, at any time, withdraw that reservation by notification to the Secretary-General.

Article 17

1. This Convention shall be open for signature at Rome on 10 March 1988 by States participating in the International Conference on the Suppression of Unlawful Acts against the Safety of Maritime Navigation and at the Headquarters of the Organization by all States from 14 March 1988 to 9 March 1989. It shall thereafter remain open for accession.

2. States may express their consent to be bound by this Convention by:

(*a*)   signature without reservation as to ratification, acceptance or approval; or (*b*)   signature subject to ratification, acceptance or approval, followed by ratification, acceptance or approval; or

(*c*)   accession.

3. Ratification, acceptance, approval or accession shall be effected by the deposit of an instrument to that effect with the Secretary-General.

Article 18

1. This Convention shall enter into force ninety days following the date on which fifteen States have either signed it without reservation as to ratification, acceptance or approval, or have deposited an instrument of ratification, acceptance, approval or accession in respect thereof.

2. For a State which deposits an instrument of ratification, acceptance, approval or accession in respect of this Convention after the conditions for entry into force thereof have been met, the ratification, acceptance, approval or accession shall take effect ninety days after the date of such deposit.

Article 19

1. This Convention may be denounced by any State Party at any time after the expiry of one year from the date on which this Convention enters into force for that State.

2. Denunciation shall be effected by the deposit of an instrument of denunciation with the Secretary-General.

3. A denunciation shall take effect one year, or such longer period as may be specified in the instrument of denunciation, after the receipt of the instrument of denunciation by the Secretary-General.

Article 20

1. A conference for the purpose of revising or amending this Convention may be convened by the Organization.

2. The Secretary-General shall convene a conference of the States

Parties to this Convention for revising or amending the Convention, at the request of one third of the States Parties, or ten States Parties, whichever is the higher figure.

3. Any instrument of ratification, acceptance, approval or accession deposited after the date of entry into force of an amendment to this Convention shall be deemed to apply to the Convention as amended.

Article 21

1. This Convention shall be deposited with the Secretary-General.

2. The Secretary-General shall:

(*a*)   inform all States which have signed this Convention or acceded thereto, and all Members of the Organization, of:

(i)   each new signature or deposit of an instrument of ratification, acceptance, approval or accession together with the date thereof;

(ii)   . the date of the entry into force of this Convention;

(iii)   the deposit of any instrument of denunciation of this Convention together with the date on which it is received and the date on which the denunciation takes effect;

(iv)   the receipt of any declaration or notification made under this Convention;

(*b*)   transmit certified true copies of this Convention to all States which have signed this Convention or acceded thereto.

3. As soon as this Convention enters into force, a certified true copy thereof shall be transmitted by the Depositary to the Secretary-General of the United Nations for registration and publication in accordance with Article 102 of the Charter of the United Nations.

Article 22

This Convention is established in a single original in the Arabic, Chinese, English, French, Russian and Spanish languages, each text being equally authentic.

IN WITNESS WHEREOF the undersigned being duly authorized by their respective Governments for that purpose have signed this Convention.

DONE AT ROME this tenth day of March one thousand nine hundred and eighty-eight.

---

9. Protocol for the Suppression of Unlawful Acts against the Safety of Fixed Platforms Located on the Continental Shelf

Done at Rome on 10 March 1988
In force on 1 March 1992
IMO Doc. SUA/CONF/16/Rev.2
Depositary: Secretary-General of the International Maritime Organization

THE STATES PARTIES TO THIS PROTOCOL,

BEING PARTIES to the Convention for the Suppression of Unlawful Acts against the Safety of Maritime Navigation,

RECOGNIZING that the reasons for which the Convention was elaborated also apply to fixed platforms located on the continental shelf,

TAKING ACCOUNT of the provisions of that Convention,

AFFIRMING that matters not regulated by this Protocol continue to be governed by the rules and principles of general international law,

Have agreed as follows:

Article 1

1. The provisions of Articles 5 and 7 and of Articles 10 to 16 of the Convention for the Suppression of Unlawful Acts against the Safety of Maritime Navigation (hereinafter referred to as "the Convention") shall also apply *mutatis mutandis* to the offences set forth in Article 2 of this Protocol where such offences are committed on board or against fixed platforms located on the continental shelf.

2. In cases where this Protocol does not apply pursuant to paragraph 1, it nevertheless applies when the offender or the alleged offender is found in the territory of a State Party other than the State in whose internal waters or territorial sea the fixed platform is located.

3. For the purposes of this Protocol, "fixed platform" means an artificial island, installation or structure permanently attached to the sea-bed for the purpose of exploration or exploitation of resources or for other economic purposes.

Article 2

1. Any person commits an offence if that person unlawfully and intentionally:

(*a*)   seizes or exercises control over a fixed platform by force or threat thereof or any other form of intimidation; or

(*b*)   performs an act of violence against a person on board a fixed platform if that act is likely to endanger its safety; or

(*c*)   destroys a fixed platform or causes damage to it which is likely to endanger its safety; or

(*d*)   places or causes to be placed on a fixed platform, by any means whatsoever, a device or substance which is likely to destroy that fixed platform or likely to endanger its safety; or

(*e*)   injures or kills any person in connection with the commission or the attempted commission of any of the offences set forth in subparagraphs (*a*) to (*d*).

2. Any person also commits an offence if that person:

(*a*)   attempts to commit any of the offences set forth in paragraph 1; or

(*b*)   abets the commission of any such offences perpetrated by any person or is otherwise an accomplice of a person who commits such an offence; or

(*c*)   threatens, with or without a condition, as is provided for under national law, aimed at compelling a physical or juridical person to do or refrain from doing any act, to commit any of the offences set forth in paragraph 1, subparagraphs (*b*) and (*c*), if that threat is likely to endanger the safety of the fixed platform.

Article 3

1. Each State Party shall take such measures as may be necessary to establish its jurisdiction over the offences set forth in Article 2 when the offence is committed:

(*a*)   against or on board a fixed platform while it is located on the continental shelf of that State; or

(*b*)   by a national of that State.

2. A State Party may also establish its jurisdiction over any such offence when:

(*a*)   it is committed by a stateless person whose habitual residence is in that State;

(*b*)   during its commission a national of that State is seized, threatened, injured or killed; or

(*c*)   it is committed in an attempt to compel that State to do or abstain from doing any act.

3. Any State Party which has established jurisdiction mentioned in paragraph 2 shall notify the Secretary-General of the International Maritime Organization (hereinafter referred to as "the Secretary-General"). If such State Party subsequently rescinds that jurisdiction, it shall notify the Secretary-General.

4. Each State Party shall take such measures as may be necessary to establish its jurisdiction over the offences set forth in Article 2 in cases where the alleged offender is present in its territory and it does not extradite him to any of the States Parties which have established their jurisdiction in accordance with paragraphs 1 and 2 of this Article.

5. This Protocol does not exclude any criminal jurisdiction exercised in accordance with national law.

Article 4

Nothing in this Protocol shall affect in any way the rules of international law pertaining to fixed platforms located on the continental shelf.

Article 5

1. This Protocol shall be open for signature at Rome on 10 March 1988 and at the Headquarters of the International Maritime Organization (hereinafter referred to as "the Organization") from 14 March 1988 to 9 March 1989 by any State which has signed the Convention. It shall thereafter remain open for accession.

2. States may express their consent to be bound by this Protocol by:

(*a*)   signature without reservation as to ratification, acceptance or approval; or

(*b*)   signature subject to ratification, acceptance or approval, followed by ratification, acceptance or approval; or

(*c*)   accession.

3. Ratification, acceptance, approval or accession shall be effected by the deposit of an instrument to that effect with the Secretary-General.

4. Only a State which has signed the Convention without reservation as to ratification, acceptance or approval, or has ratified, accepted, approved or acceded to the Convention may become a Party to this Protocol.

Article 6

1. This Protocol shall enter into force ninety days following the date on which three States have either signed it without reservation as to ratification, acceptance or approval, or have deposited an instrument of ratification, acceptance, approval or accession in respect thereof. However, this Protocol shall not enter into force before the Convention has entered into force.

85

2. For a State which deposits an instrument of ratification, acceptance, approval or accession in respect of this Protocol after the conditions for entry into force thereof have been met, the ratification, acceptance, approval or accession shall take effect ninety days after the date of such deposit.

Article 7

1. This Protocol may be denounced by any State Party at any time after the expiry of one year from the date on which this Protocol enters into force for that State.

2. Denunciation shall be effected by the deposit of an instrument of denunciation with the Secretary-General.

3. A denunciation shall take effect one year, or such longer period as may be specified in the instrument of denunciation, after the receipt of the instrument of denunciation by the Secretary-General.

4. A denunciation of the Convention by a State Party shall be deemed to be a denunciation of this Protocol by that Party.

Article 8

1. A conference for the purpose of revising or amending this Protocol may be convened by the Organization.

2. The Secretary-General shall convene a conference of the States Parties to this Protocol for revising or amending the Protocol, at the request of one third of the States Parties, or five States Parties, whichever is the higher figure.

3. Any instrument of ratification, acceptance, approval or accession deposited after the date of entry into force of an amendment to this Protocol shall be deemed to apply to the Protocol as amended.

Article 9

1. This Protocol shall be deposited with the Secretary-General.

2. The Secretary-General shall:

(*a*)   inform all States which have signed this Protocol or acceded thereto, and all Members of the Organization, of:

   (i)   each new signature or deposit of an instrument of ratification, acceptance, approval or accession, together with the date thereof;

   (ii)   the date of entry into force of this Protocol;

   (iii)   the deposit of any instrument of denunciation of this Protocol together with the date on which it is received and the date on which the denunciation takes effect;

   (iv)   the receipt of any declaration or notification made under this Protocol or under the Convention, concerning this Protocol;

(*b*)   transmit certified true copies of this Protocol to all States which have signed this Protocol or acceded thereto.

3. As soon as this Protocol enters into force, a certified true copy thereof shall be transmitted by the Depositary to the Secretary-General of the United Nations for registration and publication in accordance with Article 102 of the Charter of the United Nations.

Article 10

This Protocol is established in a single original in the Arabic, Chinese, English, French, Russian and Spanish languages, each text being equally authentic.

IN WITNESS WHEREOF the undersigned, being duly authorized by their respective Governments for that purpose, have signed this Protocol.

DONE AT ROME this tenth day of March one thousand nine hundred and eighty-eight.

10. Convention on the Marking of Plastic Explosives for the Purpose of Detection

Signed at Montreal on 1 March 1991
In force on 21 June 1998
U.N. Doc. S/22393
Depositary: International Civil Aviation Organization

THE STATES PARTIES TO THIS CONVENTION,

CONSCIOUS of the implications of acts of terrorism for international security;

EXPRESSING deep concern regarding terrorist acts aimed at destruction of aircraft, other means of transportation and other targets;

CONCERNED that plastic explosives have been used for such terrorist acts;

CONSIDERING that the marking of such explosives for the purpose of detection would contribute significantly to the prevention of such unlawful acts;

RECOGNIZING that for the purpose of deterring such unlawful acts there is an urgent need for an international instrument obliging States to adopt appropriate measures to ensure that plastic explosives are duly marked;

CONSIDERING United Nations Security Council Resolution 635 of 14 June 1989, and United Nations General Assembly Resolution 44/29 of 4 December 1989 urging the International Civil Aviation Organization to intensify its work on devising an international regime for the marking of plastic or sheet explosives for the purpose of detection;

BEARING IN MIND Resolution A27-8 adopted unanimously by the 27th Session of the Assembly of the International Civil Aviation Organization which endorsed with the highest and overriding priority the preparation of a new international instrument regarding the marking of plastic or sheet explosives for detection;

NOTING with satisfaction the role played by the Council of the International Civil Aviation Organization in the preparation of the Convention as well as its willingness to assume functions related to its implementation;

Have agreed as follows:

Article I

For the purposes of this Convention:

1. "Explosives" mean explosive products, commonly known as "plastic explosives", including explosives in flexible or elastic sheet form, as described in the Technical Annex to this Convention.

2. "Detection agent" means a substance as described in the Technical Annex to this Convention which is introduced into an explosive to render it detectable.

3. "Marking" means introducing into an explosive a detection agent in accordance with the Technical Annex to this Convention.

4. "Manufacture" means any process, including reprocessing, that produces explosives.

5. "Duly authorized military devices" include, but are not restricted to, shells, bombs, projectiles, mines, missiles, rockets, shaped charges, grenades and perforators manufactured exclusively for military or police purposes according to the laws and regulations of the State Party concerned.

6. "Producer State" means any State in whose territory explosives are manufactured.

Article II

Each State Party shall take the necessary and effective measures to prohibit and prevent the manufacture in its territory of unmarked explosives.

Article III

1. Each State Party shall take the necessary and effective measures to prohibit and prevent the movement into or out of its territory of unmarked explosives.

2. The preceding paragraph shall not apply in respect of movements for purposes not inconsistent with the objectives of this Convention, by authorities of a State Party performing military or police functions, of unmarked explosives under the control of that State Party in accordance with paragraph 1 of Article IV.

Article IV

1. Each State Party shall take the necessary measures to exercise strict and effective control over the possession and transfer of possession of unmarked explosives which have been manufactured in or brought into its territory prior to the entry into force of this Convention in respect of that State, so as to prevent their diversion or use for purposes inconsistent with the objectives of this Convention.

2. Each State Party shall take the necessary measures to ensure that all stocks of those explosives referred to in paragraph 1 of this Article not held by its authorities performing military or police functions are destroyed or consumed for purposes not inconsistent with the objectives of this Convention, marked or rendered permanently ineffective, within a period of three years from the entry into force of this Convention in respect of that State.

3. Each State Party shall take the necessary measures to ensure that all stocks of those explosives referred to in paragraph 1 of this Article held by its authorities performing military or police functions and that are not incorporated as an integral part of duly authorized military devices are destroyed or consumed for purposes not inconsistent with the objectives of this Convention, marked or rendered permanently ineffective, within a period of fifteen years from the entry into force of this Convention in respect of that State.

4. Each State Party shall take the necessary measures to ensure the destruction, as soon as possible, in its territory of unmarked explosives which may be discovered therein and which are not referred to in the preceding paragraphs of this Article, other than stocks of unmarked explosives held by its authorities performing military or police functions and incorporated as an integral part of duly authorized military devices at the date of the entry into force of this Convention in respect of that State.

5. Each State Party shall take the necessary measures to exercise strict and effective control over the possession and transfer of possession of the explosives referred to in paragraph II of Part 1 of the Technical Annex to this Convention so as to prevent their diversion or use for purposes inconsistent with the objectives of this Convention.

6. Each State Party shall take the necessary measures to ensure the destruction, as soon as possible, in its territory of unmarked explosives manufactured since the coming into force of this Convention in respect of that State that are not incorporated as specified in paragraph II (*d*) of Part 1 of the Technical Annex to this Convention and of unmarked explosives which no longer fall within the scope of any other sub-paragraphs of the said paragraph II.

Article V

1. There is established by this Convention an International Explosives Technical Commission (hereinafter referred to as "the Commission") consisting of not less than fifteen nor more than nineteen members appointed by the Council of the International Civil Aviation Organization (hereinafter referred to as "the Council") from among persons nominated by States Parties to this Convention.

2. The members of the Commission shall be experts having direct and substantial experience in matters relating to the manufacture or detection of, or research in, explosives.

3. Members of the Commission shall serve for a period of three years and shall be eligible for re-appointment.

4. Sessions of the Commission shall be convened at least once a year at the Headquarters of the International Civil Aviation Organization, or at such places and times as may be directed or approved by the Council.

5. The Commission shall adopt its rules of procedure, subject to the approval of the Council.

Article VI

1. The Commission shall evaluate technical developments relating to the manufacture, marking and detection of explosives.

2. The Commission, through the Council, shall report its findings to the States Parties and international organizations concerned.

3. Whenever necessary, the Commission shall make recommendations to the Council for amendments to the Technical Annex to this Convention. The Commission shall endeavour to take its decisions on such recommendations by consensus. In the absence of consensus the Commission shall take such decisions by a two-thirds majority vote of its members.

4. The Council may, on the recommendation of the Commission, propose to States Parties amendments to the Technical Annex to this Convention.

Article VII

1. Any State Party may, within ninety days from the date of notification of a proposed amendment to the Technical Annex to this Convention, transmit to the Council its comments. The Council shall communicate these comments to the Commission as soon as possible for its consideration. The Council shall invite any State Party which comments on or objects to the proposed amendment to consult the Commission.

2. The Commission shall consider the views of States Parties made pursuant to the preceding paragraph and report to the Council. The Council, after consideration of the Commission's report, and taking into account the nature of the amendment and the comments of States Parties, including producer States, may propose the amendment to all States Parties for adoption.

3. If a proposed amendment has not been objected to by five or more States Parties by means of written notification to the Council within

ninety days from the date of notification of the amendment by the Council, it shall be deemed to have been adopted, and shall enter into force one hundred and eighty days thereafter or after such other period as specified in the proposed amendment for States Parties not having expressly objected thereto.

4. States Parties having expressly objected to the proposed amendment may, subsequently, by means of the deposit of an instrument of acceptance or approval, express their consent to be bound by the provisions of the amendment.

5. If five or more States Parties have objected to the proposed amendment, the Council shall refer it to the Commission for further consideration.

6. If the proposed amendment has not been adopted in accordance with paragraph 3 of this Article, the Council may also convene a conference of all States Parties.

Article VIII

1. States Parties shall, if possible, transmit to the Council information that would assist the Commission in the discharge of its functions under paragraph 1 of Article VI.

2. States Parties shall keep the Council informed of measures they have taken to implement the provisions of this Convention. The Council shall communicate such information to all States Parties and international organizations concerned.

Article IX

The Council shall, in co-operation with States Parties and international organizations concerned, take appropriate measures to facilitate the implementation of this Convention, including the provision of technical assistance and measures for the exchange of information relating to technical developments in the marking and detection of explosives.

Article X

The Technical Annex to this Convention shall form an integral part of this Convention.

Article XI

1. Any dispute between two or more States Parties concerning the interpretation or application of this Convention which cannot be settled through negotiation shall, at the request of one of them, be submitted to arbitration. If within six months from the date of the request for arbitration the Parties are unable to agree on the organization of the arbitration, any one of those Parties may refer the dispute to the International Court of Justice by request in conformity with the Statute of the Court.

2. Each State Party may, at the time of signature, ratification, acceptance or approval of this Convention or accession thereto, declare that it does not consider itself bound by the preceding paragraph. The other States Parties shall not be bound by the preceding paragraph with respect to any State Party having made such a reservation.

3. Any State Party having made a reservation in accordance with the preceding paragraph may at any time withdraw this reservation by notification to the Depositary.

Article XII

Except as provided in Article XI no reservation may be made to this Convention.

Article XIII

1. This Convention shall be open for signature in Montreal on 1 March 1991 by States participating in the International Conference on Air Law held at Montreal from 12 February to 1 March 1991. After 1 March 1991 the Convention shall be open to all States for signature at the Headquarters of the International Civil Aviation Organization in Montreal until it enters into force in accordance with paragraph 3 of this Article. Any State which does not sign this Convention may accede to it at any time.

2. This Convention shall be subject to ratification, acceptance, approval or accession by States. Instruments of ratification, acceptance, approval or accession shall be deposited with the International Civil Aviation Organization, which is hereby designated the Depositary. When depositing its instrument of ratification, acceptance, approval or accession, each State shall declare whether or not it is a producer State.

3. This Convention shall enter into force on the sixtieth day following the date of deposit of the thirty-fifth instrument of ratification, acceptance, approval or accession with the Depositary, provided that no fewer than five such States have declared pursuant to paragraph 2 of this Article that they are producer States. Should thirty-five such instruments be deposited prior to the deposit of their instruments by five producer States, this Convention shall enter into force on the sixtieth day following the date of deposit of the instrument of ratification, acceptance, approval or accession of the fifth producer State.

4. For other States, this Convention shall enter into force sixty days following the date of deposit of their instruments of ratification, acceptance, approval or accession.

5. As soon as this Convention comes into force, it shall be registered by the Depositary pursuant to Article 102 of the Charter of the United Nations and pursuant to Article 83 of the Convention on International Civil Aviation (Chicago, 1944).

Article XIV

The Depositary shall promptly notify all signatories and States Parties of:

1. each signature of this Convention and date thereof;

2. each deposit of an instrument of ratification, acceptance, approval or accession and date thereof, giving special reference to whether the State has identified itself as a producer State;

3. the date of entry into force of this Convention;

4. the date of entry into force of any amendment to this Convention

or its Technical Annex;

     5. any denunciation made under Article XV; and

     6. any declaration made under paragraph 2 of Article XI.

Article XV

     1. Any State Party may denounce this Convention by written notification to the Depositary.

     2. Denunciation shall take effect one hundred and eighty days following the date on which notification is received by the Depositary.

     IN WITNESS WHEREOF the undersigned Plenipotentiaries, being duly authorized thereto by their Governments, have signed this Convention.

     DONE at Montreal, this first day of March, one thousand nine hundred and ninety-one, in one original, drawn up in five authentic texts in the English, French, Russian, Spanish and Arabic languages.

TECHNICAL ANNEX

PART 1: DESCRIPTION OF EXPLOSIVES

     I. The explosives referred to in paragraph 1 of Article I of this Convention are those that:

(*a*)   are formulated with one or more high explosives which in their pure form have a vapour pressure less than 10^{-4} Pa at a temperature of $25\,°C$;

(*b*)   are formulated with a binder material; and

(*c*)   are, as a mixture, malleable or flexible at normal room temperature.

     II. The following explosives, even though meeting the description of explosives in paragraph I of this Part, shall not be considered to be explosives as long as they continue to be held or used for the purposes specified below or remain incorporated as there specified, namely those explosives that:

(*a*)   are manufactured, or held, in limited quantities solely for use in duly authorized research, development or testing of new or modified explosives;

(*b*)   are manufactured, or held, in limited quantities solely for use in duly authorized training in explosives detection and/or development or testing of explosives detection equipment;

(*c*)   are manufactured, or held, in limited quantities solely for duly authorized forensic science purposes; or

(*d*)   are destined to be and are incorporated as an integral part of duly authorized military devices in the territory of the producer State within three years after the coming into force of this Convention in respect of that State. Such devices produced in this period of three years shall be deemed to be duly authorized military devices within paragraph 4 of Article IV of this Convention.

III. In this Part:

"duly authorized" in paragraph II (*a*), (*b*) and (*c*) means permitted according to the laws and regulations of the State Party concerned; and

"high explosives" include but are not restricted to cyclotetramethylenetetranitramine (HMX), pentaerythritol tetranitrate (PETN) and cyclotrimethylenetrinitramine (RDX).

PART 2: DETECTION AGENTS

A detection agent is any one of those substances set out in the following Table. Detection agents described in this Table are intended to be used to enhance the detectability of explosives by vapour detection means. In each case, the introduction of a detection agent into an explosive shall be done in such a manner as to achieve homogeneous distribution in the finished product. The minimum concentration of a detection agent in the finished product at the time of manufacture shall be as shown in the said Table.

TABLE

Name of detection agent	Molecular formula	Molecular weight	Minimum concentration
Ethylene glycol dinitrate (EGDN)	$C_2H_4(NO_3)_2$	152	0.2% by mass
2,3-Dimethyl-2, 3- dinitrobutane (DMNB)	$C_6H_{12}(NO_2)_2$	176	0.1% by mass
para-Mononitrotoluene (p-MNT)	$C_7H_7NO_2$	137	0.5% by mass
ortho-Mononitrotoluene (o-MNT)	$C_7H_7NO_2$	137	0.5% by mass

Any explosive which, as a result of its normal formulation contains any of the designated detection agents at or above the required minimum concentration level shall be deemed to be marked.

11. International Convention for the Suppression of Terrorist Bombings

Adopted by the General Assembly of the United Nations on
15 December 1997
Entry into force in accordance with Article 22
U.N. Doc. A/RES/52/164, Annex
Depositary: Secretary-General of the United Nations

THE STATES PARTIES TO THIS CONVENTION,

HAVING IN MIND the purposes and principles of the Charter of the United Nations concerning the maintenance of international peace and security and the promotion of good-neighbourliness and friendly relations and cooperation among States,

DEEPLY CONCERNED about the worldwide escalation of acts of terrorism in all its forms and manifestations,

RECALLING the Declaration on the Occasion of the Fiftieth Anniversary of the United Nations of 24 October 1995,

RECALLING ALSO the Declaration on Measures to Eliminate International Terrorism, annexed to General Assembly resolution 49/60 of 9 December 1994, in which, *inter alia*, "the States Members of the United Nations solemnly reaffirm their unequivocal condemnation of all acts, methods and practices of terrorism as criminal and unjustifiable, wherever and by whomever committed, including those which jeopardize the friendly relations among States and peoples and threaten the territorial integrity and security of States",

NOTING that the Declaration also encouraged States "to review urgently the scope of the existing international legal provisions on the prevention, repression and elimination of terrorism in all its forms and manifestations, with the aim of ensuring that there is a comprehensive legal framework covering all aspects of the matter",

RECALLING General Assembly resolution 51/210 of 17 December 1996 and the Declaration to Supplement the 1994 Declaration on Measures to Eliminate International Terrorism, annexed thereto,

NOTINGthat terrorist attacks by means of explosives or other lethal devices have become increasingly widespread,

NOTING also that existing multilateral legal provisions do not adequately address these attacks,

BEING CONVINCED of the urgent need to enhance international cooperation between States in devising and adopting effective and practical measures for the prevention of such acts of terrorism, and for the prosecution and punishment of their perpetrators,

CONSIDERING that the occurrence of such acts is a matter of grave concern to the international community as a whole,

NOTING that the activities of military forces of States are governed by rules of international law outside the framework of this Convention and that the exclusion of certain actions from the coverage of this Convention does not condone or make lawful otherwise unlawful acts, or preclude prosecution under other laws,

Have agreed as follows:

Article 1

For the purposes of this Convention:

1. "State or government facility" includes any permanent or temporary facility or conveyance that is used or occupied by representatives of a State, members of Government, the legislature or the judiciary or by officials or employees of a State or any other public authority or entity or by employees or officials of an intergovernmental organization in connection with their official duties.

2. "Infrastructure facility" means any publicly or privately owned facility providing or distributing services for the benefit of the public, such as water, sewage, energy, fuel or communications.

3. "Explosive or other lethal device" means:

(*a*)   An explosive or incendiary weapon or device that is designed, or has the capability, to cause death, serious bodily injury or substantial material damage; or

(*b*)   A weapon or device that is designed, or has the capability, to cause death, serious bodily injury or substantial material damage through the release, dissemination or impact of toxic chemicals, biological agents or toxins or similar substances or radiation or radioactive material.

4. "Military forces of a State" means the armed forces of a State which are organized, trained and equipped under its internal law for the primary purpose of national defence or security, and persons acting in support of those armed forces who are under their formal command, control and responsibility.

5. "Place of public use" means those parts of any building, land, street, waterway or other location that are accessible or open to members of the public, whether continuously, periodically or occasionally, and encompasses any commercial, business, cultural, historical, educational, religious, governmental, entertainment, recreational or similar place that is so accessible or open to the public.

6. "Public transportation system" means all facilities, conveyances and instrumentalities, whether publicly or privately owned, that are used in or for publicly available services for the transportation of persons or cargo.

Article 2

1. Any person commits an offence within the meaning of this Convention if that person unlawfully and intentionally delivers, places, discharges or detonates an explosive or other lethal device in, into or against a place of public use, a State or government facility, a public transportation system or an infrastructure facility:

(*a*)   With the intent to cause death or serious bodily injury; or

101

(*b*)   With the intent to cause extensive destruction of such a place, facility or system, where such destruction results in or is likely to result in major economic loss.

2. Any person also commits an offence if that person attempts to commit an offence as set forth in paragraph 1.

3. Any person also commits an offence if that person:

(*a*)   Participates as an accomplice in an offence as set forth in paragraph 1 or 2; or

(*b*)   Organizes or directs others to commit an offence as set forth in paragraph 1 or 2; or

(*c*)   In any other way contributes to the commission of one or more offences as set forth in paragraph 1 or 2 by a group of persons acting with a common purpose; such contribution shall be intentional and either be made with the aim of furthering the general criminal activity or purpose of the group or be made in the knowledge of the intention of the group to commit the offence or offences concerned.

Article 3

This Convention shall not apply where the offence is committed within a single State, the alleged offender and the victims are nationals of that State, the alleged offender is found in the territory of that State and no other State has a basis under Article 6, paragraph 1, or Article 6, paragraph 2, of this Convention to exercise jurisdiction, except that the provisions of Articles 10 to 15 shall, as appropriate, apply in those cases.

Article 4

Each State Party shall adopt such measures as may be necessary:

(*a*)   To establish as criminal offences under its domestic law the offences set forth in Article 2 of this Convention;

(*b*) To make those offences punishable by appropriate penalties which take into account the grave nature of those offences.

Article 5

Each State Party shall adopt such measures as may be necessary, including, where appropriate, domestic legislation, to ensure that criminal acts within the scope of this Convention, in particular where they are intended or calculated to provoke a state of terror in the general public or in a group of persons or particular persons, are under no circumstances justifiable by considerations of a political, philosophical, ideological, racial, ethnic, religious or other similar nature and are punished by penalties consistent with their grave nature.

Article 6

1. Each State Party shall take such measures as may be necessary to establish its jurisdiction over the offences set forth in Article 2 when:

(*a*) The offence is committed in the territory of that State; or

(*b*) The offence is committed on board a vessel flying the flag of that State or an aircraft which is registered under the laws of that State at the time the offence is committed; or

(*c*) The offence is committed by a national of that State.

2. A State Party may also establish its jurisdiction over any such offence when:

(*a*) The offence is committed against a national of that State; or

(*b*) The offence is committed against a State or government facility of that State abroad, including an embassy or other diplomatic or consular premises of that State; or

(*c*) The offence is committed by a stateless person who has his or her habitual residence in the territory of that State; or (*d*)   The offence is committed in an attempt to compel that State to do or abstain from doing any act; or

(*e*)   The offence is committed on board an aircraft which is operated by the Government of that State.

3. Upon ratifying, accepting, approving or acceding to this Convention, each State Party shall notify the Secretary-General of the United Nations of the jurisdiction it has established in accordance with paragraph 2 under its domestic law. Should any change take place, the State Party concerned shall immediately notify the Secretary-General.

4. Each State Party shall likewise take such measures as may be necessary to establish its jurisdiction over the offences set forth in Article 2 in cases where the alleged offender is present in its territory and it does not extradite that person to any of the States Parties which have established their jurisdiction in accordance with paragraph 1 or 2.

5. This Convention does not exclude the exercise of any criminal jurisdiction established by a State Party in accordance with its domestic law.

Article 7

1. Upon receiving information that a person who has committed or who is alleged to have committed an offence as set forth in Article 2 may be present in its territory, the State Party concerned shall take such measures as may be necessary under its domestic law to investigate the facts contained in the information.

2. Upon being satisfied that the circumstances so warrant, the State Party in whose territory the offender or alleged offender is present shall take the appropriate measures under its domestic law so as to ensure that person's presence for the purpose of prosecution or extradition.

3. Any person regarding whom the measures referred to in paragraph 2 are being taken shall be entitled to:

(*a*)   Communicate without delay with the nearest appropriate representative of the State of which that person is a national or which is otherwise entitled to protect that person's rights or, if that person is a stateless person, the State in the territory of which that person habitually resides;

(*b*)   Be visited by a representative of that State;

(*c*)   Be informed of that person's rights under subparagraphs (*a*) and (*b*).

4. The rights referred to in paragraph 3 shall be exercised in conformity with the laws and regulations of the State in the territory of which the offender or alleged offender is present, subject to the provision that the said laws and regulations must enable full effect to be given to the purposes for which the rights accorded under paragraph 3 are intended.

5. The provisions of paragraphs 3 and 4 shall be without prejudice to the right of any State Party having a claim to jurisdiction in accordance with Article 6, subparagraph 1 (*c*) or 2 (*c*), to invite the International Committee of the Red Cross to communicate with and visit the alleged offender.

6. When a State Party, pursuant to this Article, has taken a person into custody, it shall immediately notify, directly or through the Secretary-General of the United Nations, the States Parties which have established jurisdiction in accordance with Article 6, paragraphs 1 and 2, and, if it considers it advisable, any other interested States Parties, of the fact that such person is in custody and of the circumstances which warrant that person's detention. The State which makes the investigation contemplated in paragraph 1 shall promptly inform the said States Parties of its findings and shall indicate whether it intends to exercise jurisdiction.

Article 8

1. The State Party in the territory of which the alleged offender is present shall, in cases to which Article 6 applies, if it does not extradite that person, be obliged, without exception whatsoever and whether or not the offence was committed in its territory, to submit the case without undue delay to its competent authorities for the purpose of prosecution, through proceedings in accordance with the laws of that State. Those

authorities shall take their decision in the same manner as in the case of any other offence of a grave nature under the law of that State.

2. Whenever a State Party is permitted under its domestic law to extradite or otherwise surrender one of its nationals only upon the condition that the person will be returned to that State to serve the sentence imposed as a result of the trial or proceeding for which the extradition or surrender of the person was sought, and this State and the State seeking the extradition of the person agree with this option and other terms they may deem appropriate, such a conditional extradition or surrender shall be sufficient to discharge the obligation set forth in paragraph 1.

Article 9

1. The offences set forth in Article 2 shall be deemed to be included as extraditable offences in any extradition treaty existing between any of the States Parties before the entry into force of this Convention. States Parties undertake to include such offences as extraditable offences in every extradition treaty to be subsequently concluded between them.

2. When a State Party which makes extradition conditional on the existence of a treaty receives a request for extradition from another State Party with which it has no extradition treaty, the requested State Party may, at its option, consider this Convention as a legal basis for extradition in respect of the offences set forth in Article 2. Extradition shall be subject to the other conditions provided by the law of the requested State.

3. States Parties which do not make extradition conditional on the existence of a treaty shall recognize the offences set forth in Article 2 as extraditable offences between themselves, subject to the conditions provided by the law of the requested State.

4. If necessary, the offences set forth in Article 2 shall be treated, for the purposes of extradition between States Parties, as if they had been committed not only in the place in which they occurred but also in the territory of the States that have established jurisdiction in accordance with Article 6, paragraphs 1 and 2.

5. The provisions of all extradition treaties and arrangements

between States Parties with regard to offences set forth in Article 2 shall
be deemed to be modified as between State Parties to the extent that they
are incompatible with this Convention.

Article 10

1. States Parties shall afford one another the greatest measure of
assistance in connection with investigations or criminal or extradition
proceedings brought in respect of the offences set forth in Article 2,
including assistance in obtaining evidence at their disposal necessary for
the proceedings.

2. States Parties shall carry out their obligations under paragraph 1
in conformity with any treaties or other arrangements on mutual legal
assistance that may exist between them. In the absence of such treaties or
arrangements, States Parties shall afford one another assistance in
accordance with their domestic law.

Article 11

None of the offences set forth in Article 2 shall be regarded, for the
purposes of extradition or mutual legal assistance, as a political offence or
as an offence connected with a political offence or as an offence inspired
by political motives. Accordingly, a request for extradition or for mutual
legal assistance based on such an offence may not be refused on the sole
ground that it concerns a political offence or an offence connected with a
political offence or an offence inspired by political motives.

Article 12

Nothing in this Convention shall be interpreted as imposing an
obligation to extradite or to afford mutual legal assistance, if the requested
State Party has substantial grounds for believing that the request for
extradition for offences set forth in Article 2 or for mutual legal assistance
with respect to such offences has been made for the purpose of prosecuting
or punishing a person on account of that person's race, religion,
nationality, ethnic origin or political opinion or that compliance with the
request would cause prejudice to that person's position for any of these
reasons.

Article 13

1. A person who is being detained or is serving a sentence in the territory of one State Party whose presence in another State Party is requested for purposes of testimony, identification or otherwise providing assistance in obtaining evidence for the investigation or prosecution of offences under this Convention may be transferred if the following conditions are met:

(*a*)   The person freely gives his or her informed consent; and

(*b*)   The competent authorities of both States agree, subject to such conditions as those States may deem appropriate.

2. For the purposes of this Article:

(*a*)   The State to which the person is transferred shall have the authority and obligation to keep the person transferred in custody, unless otherwise requested or authorized by the State from which the person was transferred;

(*b*)   The State to which the person is transferred shall without delay implement its obligation to return the person to the custody of the State from which the person was transferred as agreed beforehand, or as otherwise agreed, by the competent authorities of both States;

(*c*)   The State to which the person is transferred shall not require the State from which the person was transferred to initiate extradition proceedings for the return of the person;

(*d*)   The person transferred shall receive credit for service of the sentence being served in the State from which he was transferred for time spent in the custody of the State to which he was transferred.

3. Unless the State Party from which a person is to be transferred in accordance with this Article so agrees, that person, whatever his or her nationality, shall not be prosecuted or detained or subjected to any other restriction of his or her personal liberty in the territory of the State to which that person is transferred in respect of acts or convictions anterior

to his or her departure from the territory of the State from which such person was transferred.

Article 14

Any person who is taken into custody or regarding whom any other measures are taken or proceedings are carried out pursuant to this Convention shall be guaranteed fair treatment, including enjoyment of all rights and guarantees in conformity with the law of the State in the territory of which that person is present and applicable provisions of international law, including international law of human rights.

Article 15

States Parties shall cooperate in the prevention of the offences set forth in Article 2, particularly:

(a)   By taking all practicable measures, including, if necessary, adapting their domestic legislation, to prevent and counter preparations in their respective territories for the commission of those offences within or outside their territories, including measures to prohibit in their territories illegal activities of persons, groups and organizations that encourage, instigate, organize, knowingly finance or engage in the perpetration of offences as set forth in Article 2;

(b)   By exchanging accurate and verified information in accordance with their national law, and coordinating administrative and other measures taken as appropriate to prevent the commission of offences as set forth in Article 2;

(c)   Where appropriate, through research and development regarding methods of detection of explosives and other harmful substances that can cause death or bodily injury, consultations on the development of standards for marking explosives in order to identify their origin in post-blast investigations, exchange of information on preventive measures, cooperation and transfer of technology, equipment and related materials.

Article 16

The State Party where the alleged offender is prosecuted shall, in accordance with its domestic law or applicable procedures, communicate the final outcome of the proceedings to the Secretary-General of the United Nations, who shall transmit the information to the other States Parties.

Article 17

The States Parties shall carry out their obligations under this Convention in a manner consistent with the principles of sovereign equality and territorial integrity of States and that of non-intervention in the domestic affairs of other States.

Article 18

Nothing in this Convention entitles a State Party to undertake in the territory of another State Party the exercise of jurisdiction and performance of functions which are exclusively reserved for the authorities of that other State Party by its domestic law.

Article 19

1. Nothing in this Convention shall affect other rights, obligations and responsibilities of States and individuals under international law, in particular the purposes and principles of the Charter of the United Nations and international humanitarian law.

2. The activities of armed forces during an armed conflict, as those terms are understood under international humanitarian law, which are governed by that law, are not governed by this Convention, and the activities undertaken by military forces of a State in the exercise of their official duties, inasmuch as they are governed by other rules of international law, are not governed by this Convention.

Article 20

1. Any dispute between two or more States Parties concerning the interpretation or application of this Convention which cannot be settled

through negotiation within a reasonable time shall, at the request of one of them, be submitted to arbitration. If, within six months from the date of the request for arbitration, the parties are unable to agree on the organization of the arbitration, any one of those parties may refer the dispute to the International Court of Justice, by application, in conformity with the Statute of the Court.

2. Each State may at the time of signature, ratification, acceptance or approval of this Convention or accession thereto declare that it does not consider itself bound by paragraph 1. The other States Parties shall not be bound by paragraph 1 with respect to any State Party which has made such a reservation.

3. Any State which has made a reservation in accordance with paragraph 2 may at any time withdraw that reservation by notification to the Secretary-General of the United Nations.

Article 21

1. This Convention shall be open for signature by all States from 12 January 1998 until 31 December 1999 at United Nations Headquarters in New York.

2. This Convention is subject to ratification, acceptance or approval. The instruments of ratification, acceptance or approval shall be deposited with the Secretary-General of the United Nations.

3. This Convention shall be open to accession by any State. The instruments of accession shall be deposited with the Secretary-General of the United Nations.

Article 22

1. This Convention shall enter into force on the thirtieth day following the date of the deposit of the twenty-second instrument of ratification, acceptance, approval or accession with the Secretary-General of the United Nations.

2. For each State ratifying, accepting, approving or acceding to the

111

Convention after the deposit of the twenty-second instrument of ratification, acceptance, approval or accession, the Convention shall enter into force on the thirtieth day after deposit by such State of its instrument of ratification, acceptance, approval or accession.

Article 23

1. Any State Party may denounce this Convention by written notification to the Secretary-General of the United Nations.

2. Denunciation shall take effect one year following the date on which notification is received by the Secretary-General of the United Nations.

Article 24

The original of this Convention, of which the Arabic, Chinese, English, French, Russian and Spanish texts are equally authentic, shall be deposited with the Secretary-General of the United Nations, who shall send certified copies thereof to all States.

IN WITNESS WHEREOF, the undersigned, being duly authorized thereto by their respective Governments, have signed this Convention, opened for signature at New York on 12 January 1998.

12. International Convention for the Suppression of the Financing of Terrorism

*Adopted by the General Assembly of the United Nations on
9 December 1999
Entry into force in accordance with Article 26
U.N. Doc. A/RES/54/109, Annex
Depositary: Secretary-General of the United Nations*

THE STATES PARTIES TO THIS CONVENTION,

BEARING IN MIND the purposes and principles of the Charter of the United Nations concerning the maintenance of international peace and security and the promotion of good-neighbourliness and friendly relations and cooperation among States,

DEEPLY CONCERNED about the worldwide escalation of acts of terrorism in all its forms and manifestations,

RECALLING the Declaration on the Occasion of the Fiftieth Anniversary of the United Nations, contained in General Assembly resolution 50/6 of 24 October 1995,

RECALLING ALSO all the relevant General Assembly resolutions on the matter, including resolution 49/60 of 9 December 1994 and its annex on the Declaration on Measures to Eliminate International Terrorism, in which the States Members of the United Nations solemnly reaffirmed their unequivocal condemnation of all acts, methods and practices of terrorism as criminal and unjustifiable, wherever and by whomever committed, including those which jeopardize the friendly relations among States and peoples and threaten the territorial integrity and security of States,

NOTING that the Declaration on Measures to Eliminate International Terrorism also encouraged States to review urgently the scope of the existing international legal provisions on the prevention, repression and elimination of terrorism in all its forms and manifestations, with the aim of ensuring that there is a comprehensive legal framework covering all aspects of the matter,

RECALLING General Assembly resolution 51/210 of 17 December 1996, paragraph 3, subparagraph (f), in which the Assembly called upon all States to take steps to prevent and counteract, through appropriate domestic measures, the financing of terrorists and terrorist organizations, whether such financing is direct or indirect through organizations which also have or claim to have charitable, social or cultural goals or which are also engaged in unlawful activities such as illicit arms trafficking, drug dealing and racketeering, including the exploitation of persons for purposes of funding terrorist activities, and in particular to consider, where appropriate, adopting regulatory measures to prevent and counteract movements of funds suspected to be intended for terrorist purposes without impeding in any way the freedom of legitimate capital movements and to intensify the exchange of information concerning international movements of such funds,

RECALLING ALSO General Assembly resolution 52/165 of 15 December 1997, in which the Assembly called upon States to consider, in particular, the implementation of the measures set out in paragraphs 3 (a) to (f) of its resolution 51/210 of 17 December 1996,

RECALLING FURTHER General Assembly resolution 53/108 of 8 December 1998, in which the Assembly decided that the Ad Hoc Committee established by General Assembly resolution 51/210 of 17 December 1996 should elaborate a draft international convention for the suppression of terrorist financing to supplement related existing international instruments,

CONSIDERING that the financing of terrorism is a matter of grave concern to the international community as a whole,

NOTING that the number and seriousness of acts of international terrorism depend on the financing that terrorists may obtain,

NOTING ALSO that existing multilateral legal instruments do not expressly address such financing,

BEING CONVINCED of the urgent need to enhance international cooperation among States in devising and adopting effective measures for

114

the prevention of the financing of terrorism, as well as for its suppression through the prosecution and punishment of its perpetrators,

HAVE AGREED AS FOLLOWS:

Article 1

For the purposes of this Convention:

1. "Funds" means assets of every kind, whether tangible or intangible, movable or immovable, however acquired, and legal documents or instruments in any form, including electronic or digital, evidencing title to, or interest in, such assets, including, but not limited to, bank credits, travellers cheques, bank cheques, money orders, shares, securities, bonds, drafts, letters of credit.

2. "A State or governmental facility" means any permanent or temporary facility or conveyance that is used or occupied by representatives of a State, members of Government, the legislature or the judiciary or by officials or employees of a State or any other public authority or entity or by employees or officials of an intergovernmental organization in connection with their official duties.

3. "Proceeds" means any funds derived from or obtained, directly or indirectly, through the commission of an offence set forth in Article 2.

Article 2

1. Any person commits an offence within the meaning of this Convention if that person by any means, directly or indirectly, unlawfully and wilfully, provides or collects funds with the intention that they should be used or in the knowledge that they are to be used, in full or in part, in order to carry out:

(a) An act which constitutes an offence within the scope of and as defined in one of the treaties listed in the annex; or

(b) Any other act intended to cause death or serious bodily injury to a civilian, or to any other person not taking an active part in the hostilities in a situation of armed conflict, when the purpose of such

115

act, by its nature or context, is to intimidate a population, or to compel a government or an international organization to do or to abstain from doing any act.

2. *(a)* On depositing its instrument of ratification, acceptance, approval or accession, a State Party which is not a party to a treaty listed in the annex may declare that, in the application of this Convention to the State Party, the treaty shall be deemed not to be included in the annex referred to in paragraph 1, subparagraph (a). The declaration shall cease to have effect as soon as the treaty enters into force for the State Party, which shall notify the depositary of this fact;

(b) When a State Party ceases to be a party to a treaty listed in the annex, it may make a declaration as provided for in this Article, with respect to that treaty.

3. For an act to constitute an offence set forth in paragraph 1, it shall not be necessary that the funds were actually used to carry out an offence referred to in paragraph 1, subparagraphs (a) or (b).

4. Any person also commits an offence if that person attempts to commit an offence as set forth in paragraph 1 of this Article.

5. Any person also commits an offence if that person:

(a) Participates as an accomplice in an offence as set forth in paragraph 1 or 4 of this Article;

(b) Organizes or directs others to commit an offence as set forth in paragraph 1 or 4 of this Article;

(c) Contributes to the commission of one or more offences as set forth in paragraphs 1 or 4 of this Article by a group of persons acting with a common purpose. Such contribution shall be intentional and shall either:

(i) Be made with the aim of furthering the criminal activity or criminal purpose of the group, where such activity or purpose involves the commission of an offence as set forth in paragraph 1 of this Article; or

(ii)   Be made in the knowledge of the intention of the group to commit an offence as set forth in paragraph 1 of this Article.

Article 3

This Convention shall not apply where the offence is committed within a single State, the alleged offender is a national of that State and is present in the territory of that State and no other State has a basis under Article 7, paragraph 1, or Article 7, paragraph 2, to exercise jurisdiction, except that the provisions of Articles 12 to 18 shall, as appropriate, apply in those cases.

Article 4

Each State Party shall adopt such measures as may be necessary:

(a)   To establish as criminal offences under its domestic law the offences set forth in Article 2;

(b)   To make those offences punishable by appropriate penalties which take into account the grave nature of the offences.

Article 5

1. Each State Party, in accordance with its domestic legal principles, shall take the necessary measures to enable a legal entity located in its territory or organized under its laws to be held liable when a person responsible for the management or control of that legal entity has, in that capacity, committed an offence set forth in Article 2. Such liability may be criminal, civil or administrative.

2. Such liability is incurred without prejudice to the criminal liability of individuals having committed the offences.

3. Each State Party shall ensure, in particular, that legal entities liable in accordance with paragraph 1 above are subject to effective, proportionate and dissuasive criminal, civil or administrative sanctions. Such sanctions may include monetary sanctions.

Article 6

Each State Party shall adopt such measures as may be necessary, including, where appropriate, domestic legislation, to ensure that criminal acts within the scope of this Convention are under no circumstances justifiable by considerations of a political, philosophical, ideological, racial, ethnic, religious or other similar nature.

Article 7

1. Each State Party shall take such measures as may be necessary to establish its jurisdiction over the offences set forth in Article 2 when:

(a)   The offence is committed in the territory of that State;

(b)   The offence is committed on board a vessel flying the flag of that State or an aircraft registered under the laws of that State at the time the offence is committed;

(c)   The offence is committed by a national of that State.

2. A State Party may also establish its jurisdiction over any such offence when:

(a)   The offence was directed towards or resulted in the carrying out of an offence referred to in Article 2, paragraph 1, subparagraph (a) or (b), in the territory of or against a national of that State;

(b)   The offence was directed towards or resulted in the carrying out of an offence referred to in Article 2, paragraph 1, subparagraph (a) or (b), against a State or government facility of that State abroad, including diplomatic or consular premises of that State;

(c)   The offence was directed towards or resulted in an offence referred to in Article 2, paragraph 1, subparagraph (a) or (b), committed in an attempt to compel that State to do or abstain from doing any act;

(d)   The offence is committed by a stateless person who has his or her habitual residence in the territory of that State;

(e)   The offence is committed on board an aircraft which is operated by
the Government of that State.

3. Upon ratifying, accepting, approving or acceding to this
Convention, each State Party shall notify the Secretary-General of the
United Nations of the jurisdiction it has established in accordance with
paragraph 2. Should any change take place, the State Party concerned shall
immediately notify the Secretary-General.

4. Each State Party shall likewise take such measures as may be
necessary to establish its jurisdiction over the offences set forth in Article
2 in cases where the alleged offender is present in its territory and it does
not extradite that person to any of the States Parties that have established
their jurisdiction in accordance with paragraphs 1 or 2.

5. When more than one State Party claims jurisdiction over the
offences set forth in Article 2, the relevant States Parties shall strive to
coordinate their actions appropriately, in particular concerning the
conditions for prosecution and the modalities for mutual legal assistance.

6. Without prejudice to the norms of general international law, this
Convention does not exclude the exercise of any criminal jurisdiction
established by a State Party in accordance with its domestic law.

Article 8

1. Each State Party shall take appropriate measures, in accordance
with its domestic legal principles, for the identification, detection and
freezing or seizure of any funds used or allocated for the purpose of
committing the offences set forth in Article 2 as well as the proceeds
derived from such offences, for purposes of possible forfeiture.

2. Each State Party shall take appropriate measures, in accordance
with its domestic legal principles, for the forfeiture of funds used or
allocated for the purpose of committing the offences set forth in Article 2
and the proceeds derived from such offences.

3. Each State Party concerned may give consideration to concluding
agreements on the sharing with other States Parties, on a regular or case-
by-case basis, of the funds derived from the forfeitures referred to in this
Article.

4. Each State Party shall consider establishing mechanisms whereby the funds derived from the forfeitures referred to in this Article are utilized to compensate the victims of offences referred to in Article 2, paragraph 1, subparagraph (a) or (b), or their families.

5. The provisions of this Article shall be implemented without prejudice to the rights of third parties acting in good faith.

Article 9

1. Upon receiving information that a person who has committed or who is alleged to have committed an offence set forth in Article 2 may be present in its territory, the State Party concerned shall take such measures as may be necessary under its domestic law to investigate the facts contained in the information.

2. Upon being satisfied that the circumstances so warrant, the State Party in whose territory the offender or alleged offender is present shall take the appropriate measures under its domestic law so as to ensure that person's presence for the purpose of prosecution or extradition.

3. Any person regarding whom the measures referred to in paragraph 2 are being taken shall be entitled to:

(a)   Communicate without delay with the nearest appropriate representative of the State of which that person is a national or which is otherwise entitled to protect that person's rights or, if that person is a stateless person, the State in the territory of which that person habitually resides;

(b)   Be visited by a representative of that State;

(c)   Be informed of that person's rights under subparagraphs (a) and (b).

4. The rights referred to in paragraph 3 shall be exercised in conformity with the laws and regulations of the State in the territory of which the offender or alleged offender is present, subject to the provision that the said laws and regulations must enable full effect to be given to the purposes for which the rights accorded under paragraph 3 are intended.

5. The provisions of paragraphs 3 and 4 shall be without prejudice to the right of any State Party having a claim to jurisdiction in accordance with Article 7, paragraph 1, subparagraph (b), or paragraph 2, subparagraph (b), to invite the International Committee of the Red Cross to communicate with and visit the alleged offender.

6. When a State Party, pursuant to the present Article, has taken a person into custody, it shall immediately notify, directly or through the Secretary-General of the United Nations, the States Parties which have established jurisdiction in accordance with Article 7, paragraph 1 or 2, and, if it considers it advisable, any other interested States Parties, of the fact that such person is in custody and of the circumstances which warrant that person's detention. The State which makes the investigation contemplated in paragraph 1 shall promptly inform the said States Parties of its findings and shall indicate whether it intends to exercise jurisdiction.

Article 10

1. The State Party in the territory of which the alleged offender is present shall, in cases to which Article 7 applies, if it does not extradite that person, be obliged, without exception whatsoever and whether or not the offence was committed in its territory, to submit the case without undue delay to its competent authorities for the purpose of prosecution, through proceedings in accordance with the laws of that State. Those authorities shall take their decision in the same manner as in the case of any other offence of a grave nature under the law of that State.

2. Whenever a State Party is permitted under its domestic law to extradite or otherwise surrender one of its nationals only upon the condition that the person will be returned to that State to serve the sentence imposed as a result of the trial or proceeding for which the extradition or surrender of the person was sought, and this State and the State seeking the extradition of the person agree with this option and other terms they may deem appropriate, such a conditional extradition or surrender shall be sufficient to discharge the obligation set forth in paragraph 1.

Article 11

1. The offences set forth in Article 2 shall be deemed to be included as extraditable offences in any extradition treaty existing between any of the States Parties before the entry into force of this Convention. States Parties undertake to include such offences as extraditable offences in every extradition treaty to be subsequently concluded between them.

2. When a State Party which makes extradition conditional on the existence of a treaty receives a request for extradition from another State Party with which it has no extradition treaty, the requested State Party may, at its option, consider this Convention as a legal basis for extradition in respect of the offences set forth in Article 2. Extradition shall be subject to the other conditions provided by the law of the requested State.

3. States Parties which do not make extradition conditional on the existence of a treaty shall recognize the offences set forth in Article 2 as extraditable offences between themselves, subject to the conditions provided by the law of the requested State.

4. If necessary, the offences set forth in Article 2 shall be treated, for the purposes of extradition between States Parties, as if they had been committed not only in the place in which they occurred but also in the territory of the States that have established jurisdiction in accordance with Article 7, paragraphs 1 and 2.

5. The provisions of all extradition treaties and arrangements between States Parties with regard to offences set forth in Article 2 shall be deemed to be modified as between States Parties to the extent that they are incompatible with this Convention.

Article 12

1. States Parties shall afford one another the greatest measure of assistance in connection with criminal investigations or criminal or extradition proceedings in respect of the offences set forth in Article 2, including assistance in obtaining evidence in their possession necessary for the proceedings.

2. States Parties may not refuse a request for mutual legal assistance on the ground of bank secrecy.

3. The requesting Party shall not transmit nor use information or evidence furnished by the requested Party for investigations, prosecutions or proceedings other than those stated in the request without the prior consent of the requested Party.

4. Each State Party may give consideration to establishing mechanisms to share with other States Parties information or evidence needed to establish criminal, civil or administrative liability pursuant to Article 5.

5. States Parties shall carry out their obligations under paragraphs 1 and 2 in conformity with any treaties or other arrangements on mutual legal assistance or information exchange that may exist between them. In the absence of such treaties or arrangements, States Parties shall afford one another assistance in accordance with their domestic law.

Article 13

None of the offences set forth in Article 2 shall be regarded, for the purposes of extradition or mutual legal assistance, as a fiscal offence. Accordingly, States Parties may not refuse a request for extradition or for mutual legal assistance on the sole ground that it concerns a fiscal offence.

Article 14

None of the offences set forth in Article 2 shall be regarded for the purposes of extradition or mutual legal assistance as a political offence or as an offence connected with a political offence or as an offence inspired by political motives. Accordingly, a request for extradition or for mutual legal assistance based on such an offence may not be refused on the sole ground that it concerns a political offence or an offence connected with a political offence or an offence inspired by political motives.

Article 15

Nothing in this Convention shall be interpreted as imposing an obligation to extradite or to afford mutual legal assistance, if the requested

State Party has substantial grounds for believing that the request for extradition for offences set forth in Article 2 or for mutual legal assistance with respect to such offences has been made for the purpose of prosecuting or punishing a person on account of that person's race, religion, nationality, ethnic origin or political opinion or that compliance with the request would cause prejudice to that person's position for any of these reasons.

Article 16

1. A person who is being detained or is serving a sentence in the territory of one State Party whose presence in another State Party is requested for purposes of identification, testimony or otherwise providing assistance in obtaining evidence for the investigation or prosecution of offences set forth in Article 2 may be transferred if the following conditions are met:

(a)   The person freely gives his or her informed consent;

(b)   The competent authorities of both States agree, subject to such conditions as those States may deem appropriate.

2. For the purposes of the present Article:

(a)   The State to which the person is transferred shall have the authority and obligation to keep the person transferred in custody, unless otherwise requested or authorized by the State from which the person was transferred;

(b)   The State to which the person is transferred shall without delay implement its obligation to return the person to the custody of the State from which the person was transferred as agreed beforehand, or as otherwise agreed, by the competent authorities of both States;

(c)   The State to which the person is transferred shall not require the State from which the person was transferred to initiate extradition proceedings for the return of the person;

(d)   The person transferred shall receive credit for service of the sentence being served in the State from which he or she was

transferred for time spent in the custody of the State to which he or she was transferred.

3. Unless the State Party from which a person is to be transferred in accordance with the present Article so agrees, that person, whatever his or her nationality, shall not be prosecuted or detained or subjected to any other restriction of his or her personal liberty in the territory of the State to which that person is transferred in respect of acts or convictions anterior to his or her departure from the territory of the State from which such person was transferred.

Article 17

Any person who is taken into custody or regarding whom any other measures are taken or proceedings are carried out pursuant to this Convention shall be guaranteed fair treatment, including enjoyment of all rights and guarantees in conformity with the law of the State in the territory of which that person is present and applicable provisions of international law, including international human rights law.

Article 18

1. States Parties shall cooperate in the prevention of the offences set forth in Article 2 by taking all practicable measures, *inter alia*, by adapting their domestic legislation, if necessary, to prevent and counter preparations in their respective territories for the commission of those offences within or outside their territories, including:

(a)   Measures to prohibit in their territories illegal activities of persons and organizations that knowingly encourage, instigate, organize or engage in the commission of offences set forth in Article 2;

(b)   Measures requiring financial institutions and other professions involved in financial transactions to utilize the most efficient measures available for the identification of their usual or occasional customers, as well as customers in whose interest accounts are opened, and to pay special attention to unusual or suspicious transactions and report transactions suspected of stemming from a criminal activity. For this purpose, States Parties shall consider:

(i) Adopting regulations prohibiting the opening of accounts the holders or beneficiaries of which are unidentified or unidentifiable, and measures to ensure that such institutions verify the identity of the real owners of such transactions;

(ii) With respect to the identification of legal entities, requiring financial institutions, when necessary, to take measures to verify the legal existence and the structure of the customer by obtaining, either from a public register or from the customer or both, proof of incorporation, including information concerning the customer's name, legal form, address, directors and provisions regulating the power to bind the entity;

(iii) Adopting regulations imposing on financial institutions the obligation to report promptly to the competent authorities all complex, unusual large transactions and unusual patterns of transactions, which have no apparent economic or obviously lawful purpose, without fear of assuming criminal or civil liability for breach of any restriction on disclosure of information if they report their suspicions in good faith;

(iv) Requiring financial institutions to maintain, for at least five years, all necessary records on transactions, both domestic or international.

2. States Parties shall further cooperate in the prevention of offences set forth in Article 2 by considering:

(a) Measures for the supervision, including, for example, the licensing, of all money-transmission agencies;

(b) Feasible measures to detect or monitor the physical cross-border transportation of cash and bearer negotiable instruments, subject to strict safeguards to ensure proper use of information and without impeding in any way the freedom of capital movements.

3. States Parties shall further cooperate in the prevention of the offences set forth in Article 2 by exchanging accurate and verified information in accordance with their domestic law and coordinating

administrative and other measures taken, as appropriate, to prevent the commission of offences set forth in Article 2, in particular by:

(a)   Establishing and maintaining channels of communication between their competent agencies and services to facilitate the secure and rapid exchange of information concerning all aspects of offences set forth in Article 2;

(b)   Cooperating with one another in conducting inquiries, with respect to the offences set forth in Article 2, concerning:

   (i)   The identity, whereabouts and activities of persons in respect of whom reasonable suspicion exists that they are involved in such offences;

   (ii)   The movement of funds relating to the commission of such offences.

4.   States Parties may exchange information through the International Criminal Police Organization (Interpol).

Article 19

The State Party where the alleged offender is prosecuted shall, in accordance with its domestic law or applicable procedures, communicate the final outcome of the proceedings to the Secretary-General of the United Nations, who shall transmit the information to the other States Parties.

Article 20

The States Parties shall carry out their obligations under this Convention in a manner consistent with the principles of sovereign equality and territorial integrity of States and that of non-intervention in the domestic affairs of other States.

Article 21

Nothing in this Convention shall affect other rights, obligations and responsibilities of States and individuals under international law, in particular the purposes of the Charter of the United Nations, international humanitarian law and other relevant conventions.

Article 22

Nothing in this Convention entitles a State Party to undertake in the territory of another State Party the exercise of jurisdiction or performance of functions which are exclusively reserved for the authorities of that other State Party by its domestic law.

Article 23

1. The annex may be amended by the addition of relevant treaties that:

(a) Are open to the participation of all States;

(b) Have entered into force;

(c) Have been ratified, accepted, approved or acceded to by at least twenty-two States Parties to the present Convention.

2. After the entry into force of this Convention, any State Party may propose such an amendment. Any proposal for an amendment shall be communicated to the depositary in written form. The depositary shall notify proposals that meet the requirements of paragraph 1 to all States Parties and seek their views on whether the proposed amendment should be adopted.

3. The proposed amendment shall be deemed adopted unless one third of the States Parties object to it by a written notification not later than 180 days after its circulation.

4. The adopted amendment to the annex shall enter into force 30 days after the deposit of the twenty-second instrument of ratification, acceptance or approval of such amendment for all those States Parties having deposited such an instrument. For each State Party ratifying, accepting or approving the amendment after the deposit of the twenty-second instrument, the amendment shall enter into force on the thirtieth day after deposit by such State Party of its instrument of ratification, acceptance or approval.

Article 24

1. Any dispute between two or more States Parties concerning the interpretation or application of this Convention which cannot be settled through negotiation within a reasonable time shall, at the request of one of them, be submitted to arbitration. If, within six months from the date of the request for arbitration, the parties are unable to agree on the organization of the arbitration, any one of those parties may refer the dispute to the International Court of Justice, by application, in conformity with the Statute of the Court.

2. Each State may at the time of signature, ratification, acceptance or approval of this Convention or accession thereto declare that it does not consider itself bound by paragraph 1. The other States Parties shall not be bound by paragraph 1 with respect to any State Party which has made such a reservation.

3. Any State which has made a reservation in accordance with paragraph 2 may at any time withdraw that reservation by notification to the Secretary-General of the United Nations.

Article 25

1. This Convention shall be open for signature by all States from 10 January 2000 to 31 December 2001 at United Nations Headquarters in New York.

2. This Convention is subject to ratification, acceptance or approval. The instruments of ratification, acceptance or approval shall be deposited with the Secretary-General of the United Nations.

3. This Convention shall be open to accession by any State. The instruments of accession shall be deposited with the Secretary-General of the United Nations.

Article 26

1. This Convention shall enter into force on the thirtieth day following the date of the deposit of the twenty-second instrument of ratification, acceptance, approval or accession with the Secretary-General of the United Nations.

2. For each State ratifying, accepting, approving or acceding to the Convention after the deposit of the twenty-second instrument of ratification, acceptance, approval or accession, the Convention shall enter into force on the thirtieth day after deposit by such State of its instrument of ratification, acceptance, approval or accession.

Article 27

1. Any State Party may denounce this Convention by written notification to the Secretary-General of the United Nations.

2. Denunciation shall take effect one year following the date on which notification is received by the Secretary-General of the United Nations.

Article 28

The original of this Convention, of which the Arabic, Chinese, English, French, Russian and Spanish texts are equally authentic, shall be deposited with the Secretary-General of the United Nations who shall send certified copies thereof to all States.

IN WITNESS WHEREOF, the undersigned, being duly authorized thereto by their respective Governments, have signed this Convention, opened for signature at United Nations Headquarters in New York on 10 January 2000.

Annex

1.   Convention for the Suppression of Unlawful Seizure of Aircraft, done at The Hague on 16 December 1970.

2.   Convention for the Suppression of Unlawful Acts against the Safety of Civil Aviation, done at Montreal on 23 September 1971.

3.   Convention on the Prevention and Punishment of Crimes against Internationally Protected Persons, including Diplomatic Agents, adopted by the General Assembly of the United Nations on 14 December 1973.

4.   International Convention against the Taking of Hostages, adopted by the General Assembly of the United Nations on 17 December 1979.

5.   Convention on the Physical Protection of Nuclear Material, adopted at Vienna on 3 March 1980.

6.   Protocol for the Suppression of Unlawful Acts of Violence at Airports Serving International Civil Aviation, supplementary to the Convention for the Suppression of Unlawful Acts against the Safety of Civil Aviation, done at Montreal on 24 February 1988.

7.   Convention for the Suppression of Unlawful Acts against the Safety of Maritime Navigation, done at Rome on 10 March 1988.

8.   Protocol for the Suppression of Unlawful Acts against the Safety of Fixed Platforms located on the Continental Shelf, done at Rome on 10 March 1988.

9.   International Convention for the Suppression of Terrorist Bombings, adopted by the General Assembly of the United Nations on 15 December 1997.

PART II

REGIONAL INSTRUMENTS

13. OAS Convention to Prevent and Punish the Acts of Terrorism Taking the Form of Crimes Against Persons and Related Extortion that are of International Significance

Concluded at Washington, D.C. on February 2, 1971
In force on 16 October 1973
United Nations, Treaty Series, vol. 1438, No. 24381
Depositary: General Secretariat of the Organization of American States

Whereas:

The defense of freedom and justice and respect for the fundamental rights of the individual that are recognized by the American Declaration of the Rights and Duties of Man and the Universal Declaration of Human Rights are primary duties of states;

The General Assembly of the Organization, in Resolution 4, of June 30, 1970, strongly condemned acts of terrorism, especially the kidnaping of persons and extortion in connection with that crime, which it declared to be serious common crimes;

Criminal acts against persons entitled to special protection under international law are occurring frequently, and those acts are of international significance because of the consequences that may flow from them for relations among states;

It is advisable to adopt general standards that will progressively develop international law as regards cooperation in the prevention and punishment of such acts; and

In the application of those standards the institution of asylum should be maintained and, likewise, the principle of nonintervention should not be impaired,

The Member States of the Organization of American States

Have agreed upon the following articles:

Article 1

The contracting states undertake to cooperate among themselves by taking all the measures that they may consider effective, under their own laws, and especially those established in this convention, to prevent and punish acts of terrorism, especially kidnaping, murder, and other assaults against the life or physical integrity of those persons to whom the state has the duty according to international law to give special protection, as well as extortion in connection with those crimes.

Article 2

For the purposes of this convention, kidnaping, murder, and other assaults against the life or personal integrity of those persons to whom the state has the duty to give special protection according to international law, as well as extortion in connection with those crimes, shall be considered common crimes of international significance, regardless of motive.

Article 3

Persons who have been charged or convicted for any of the crimes referred to in Article 2 of this convention shall be subject to extradition under the provisions of the extradition treaties in force between the parties or, in the case of states that do not make extradition dependent on the existence of a treaty, in accordance with their own laws.

In any case, it is the exclusive responsibility of the state under whose jurisdiction or protection such persons are located to determine the nature of the acts and decide whether the standards of this convention are applicable.

Article 4

Any person deprived of his freedom through the application of this convention shall enjoy the legal guarantees of due process.

Article 5

When extradition requested for one of the crimes specified in Article 2 is not in order because the person sought is a national of the requested state, or because of some other legal or constitutional impediment, that state is obliged to submit the case to its competent authorities for prosecution, as if the act had been committed in its territory. The decision of these authorities shall be communicated to the state that requested extradition. In such proceedings, the obligation established in Article 4 shall be respected.

Article 6

None of the provisions of this convention shall be interpreted so as to impair the right of asylum.

Article 7

The contracting states undertake to include the crimes referred to in Article 2 of this convention among the punishable acts giving rise to extradition in any treaty on the subject to which they agree among themselves in the future. The contracting states that do not subject extradition to the existence of a treaty with the requesting state shall consider the crimes referred to in Article 2 of this convention as crimes giving rise to extradition, according to the conditions established by the laws of the requested state.

Article 8

To cooperate in preventing and punishing the crimes contemplated in Article 2 of this convention, the contracting states accept the following obligations:

a. To take all measures within their power, and in conformity with their own laws, to prevent and impede the preparation in their respective territories of the crimes mentioned in Article 2 that are to be carried out in the territory of another contracting state.

b. To exchange information and consider effective administrative measures for the purpose of protecting the persons to whom Article 2 of this convention refers.

c. To guarantee to every person deprived of his freedom through the application of this convention every right to defend himself.

136

d.   To endeavor to have the criminal acts contemplated in this convention included in their penal laws, if not already so included.

e.   To comply most expeditiously with the requests for extradition concerning the criminal acts contemplated in this convention.

Article 9

This convention shall remain open for signature by the member states of the Organization of American States, as well as by any other state that is a member of the United Nations or any of its specialized agencies, or any state that is a party to the Statute of the International Court of Justice, or any other state that may be invited by the General Assembly of the Organization of American States to sign it.

Article 10

This convention shall be ratified by the signatory states in accordance with their respective constitutional procedures.

Article 11

The original instrument of this convention, the English, French, Portuguese, and Spanish texts of which are equally authentic, shall be deposited in the General Secretariat of the Organization of American States, which shall send certified copies to the signatory governments for purposes of ratification. The instruments of ratification shall be deposited in the General Secretariat of the Organization of American States, which shall notify the signatory governments of such deposit.

Article 12

This convention shall enter into force among the states that ratify it when they deposit their respective instruments of ratification.

Article 13

This convention shall remain in force indefinitely, but any of the contracting states may denounce it. The denunciation shall be transmitted to the General Secretariat of the Organization of American States, which shall notify the other contracting states thereof. One year following the denunciation, the convention shall cease to be in force for the denouncing state, but shall continue to be in force for the other contracting states.

IN WITNESS WHEREOF, the undersigned plenipotentiaries, having presented their full powers, which have been found to be in due and proper form, sign this convention on behalf of their respective governments, at the city of Washington this second day of February of the year one thousand nine hundred seventy-one.

---

14. European Convention on the Suppression of Terrorism

Done at Strasbourg on 27 January 1977
In force on 4 August 1978
United Nations, Treaty Series, vol. 1137, No. 17828
Depositary: Secretary-General of the Council of Europe

The member States of the Council of Europe, signatory hereto,

Considering that the aim of the Council of Europe is to achieve a greater unity between its members;

Aware of the growing concern caused by the increase in acts of terrorism;

Wishing to take effective measures to ensure that the perpetrators of such acts do not escape prosecution and punishment;

Convinced that extradition is a particularly effective measure for achieving this result,

Have agreed as follows:

Article 1

For the purposes of extradition between Contracting States, none of the following offences shall be regarded as a political offence or as an offence connected with a political offence or as an offence inspired by political motives:

(*a*)   an offence within the scope of the Convention for the Suppression of Unlawful Seizure of Aircraft, signed at The Hague on 16 December 1970;

(*b*)   an offence within the scope of the Convention for the Suppression of Unlawful Acts against the Safety of Civil Aviation, signed at Montreal on 23 September 1971;

(c)   a serious offence involving an attack against the life, physical integrity or liberty of internationally protected persons, including diplomatic agents;

(d)   an offence involving kidnapping, the taking of a hostage or serious unlawful detention;

(e)   an offence involving the use of a bomb, grenade, rocket, automatic firearm or letter or parcel bomb if this use endangers persons;

(f)   an attempt to commit any of the foregoing offences or participation as an accomplice of a person who commits or attempts to commit such an offence.

Article 2

1. For the purposes of extradition between Contracting States, a Contracting State may decide not to regard as a political offence or as an offence connected with a political offence or as an offence inspired by political motives a serious offence involving an act of violence, other than one covered by Article 1, against the life, physical integrity or liberty of a person.

2. The same shall apply to a serious offence involving an act against property, other than one covered by Article 1, if the act created a collective danger for persons.

3. The same shall apply to an attempt to commit any of the foregoing offences or participation as an accomplice of a person who commits or attempts to commit such an offence.

Article 3

The provisions of all extradition treaties and arrangements applicable between Contracting States, including the European Convention on Extradition, are modified as between Contracting States to the extent that they are incompatible with this Convention

Article 4

For the purposes of this Convention and to the extent that any offence mentioned in Article 1 or 2 is not listed as an extraditable offence in any extradition convention or treaty existing between Contracting States, it shall be deemed to be included as such therein.

Article 5

Nothing in this Convention shall be interpreted as imposing an obligation to extradite if the requested State has substantial grounds for believing that the request for extradition for an offence mentioned in Article 1 or 2 has been made for the purpose of prosecuting or punishing a person on account of his race, religion, nationality or political opinion, or that that person's position may be prejudiced for any of these reasons.

Article 6

1. Each Contracting State shall take such measures as may be necessary to establish its jurisdiction over an offence mentioned in Article 1 in the case where the suspected offender is present in its territory and it does not extradite him after receiving a request for extradition from a Contracting State whose jurisdiction is based on a rule of jurisdiction existing equally in the law of the requested State.

2. This Convention does not exclude any criminal jurisdiction exercised in accordance with national law.

Article 7

A Contracting State in whose territory a person suspected to have committed an offence mentioned in Article 1 is found and which has received a request for extradition under the conditions mentioned in Article 6, paragraph 1, shall, if it does not extradite that person, submit the case, without exception whatsoever and without undue delay, to its competent authorities for the purpose of prosecution. Those authorities shall take their decision in the same manner as in the case of any offence of a serious nature under the law of that State.

Article 8

1. Contracting States shall afford one another the widest measure of mutual assistance in criminal matters in connection with proceedings brought in respect of the offences mentioned in Article 1 or 2. The law of the requested State concerning mutual assistance in criminal matters shall apply in all cases. Nevertheless this assistance may not be refused on the sole ground that it concerns a political offence or an offence connected with a political offence or an offence inspired by political motives.

2. Nothing in this Convention shall be interpreted as imposing an obligation to afford mutual assistance if the requested State has substantial grounds for believing that the request for mutual assistance in respect of an offence mentioned in Article 1 or 2 has been made for the purpose of prosecuting or punishing a person on account of his race, religion, nationality or political opinion or that that person's position may be prejudiced for any of these reasons.

3. The provisions of all treaties and arrangements concerning mutual assistance in criminal matters applicable between Contracting States, including the European Convention on Mutual Assistance in Criminal Matters, are modified as between Contracting States to the extent that they are incompatible with this Convention.

Article 9

1. The European Committee on Crime Problems of the Council of Europe shall be kept informed regarding the application of this Convention.

2. It shall do whatever is needful to facilitate a friendly settlement of any difficulty which may arise out of its execution.

Article 10

1. Any dispute between Contracting States concerning the interpretation or application of this Convention, which has not been settled in the framework of Article 9, paragraph 2, shall, at the request of any Party to the dispute, be referred to arbitration. Each Party shall nominate an arbitrator and the two arbitrators shall nominate a referee. If any Party

has not nominated its arbitrator within the three months following the request for arbitration, he shall be nominated at the request of the other Party by the President of the European Court of Human Rights. If the latter should be a national of one of the Parties to the dispute, this duty shall be carried out by the Vice-President of the Court or, if the Vice-President is a national of one of the Parties to the dispute, by the most senior judge of the Court not being a national of one of the Parties to the dispute. The same procedure shall be observed if the arbitrators cannot agree on the choice of referee.

2. The arbitration tribunal shall lay down its own procedure. Its decisions shall be taken by majority vote. Its award shall be final.

Article 11

1. This Convention shall be open to signature by the member States of the Council of Europe. It shall be subject to ratification, acceptance or approval. Instruments of ratification, acceptance or approval shall be deposited with the Secretary General of the Council of Europe.

2. The Convention shall enter into force three months after the date of the deposit of the third instrument of ratification, acceptance or approval.

3. In respect of a signatory State ratifying, accepting or approving subsequently, the Convention shall come into force three months after the date of the deposit of its instrument of ratification, acceptance or approval.

Article 12

1. Any State may, at the time of signature or when depositing its instrument of ratification, acceptance or approval, specify the territory or territories to which this Convention shall apply.

2. Any State may, when depositing its instrument of ratification, acceptance or approval or at any later date, by declaration addressed to the Secretary General of the Council of Europe, extend this Convention to any other territory or territories specified in the declaration and for whose international relations it is responsible or on whose behalf it is authorized to give undertakings.

3. Any declaration made in pursuance of the preceding paragraph may, in respect of any territory mentioned in such declaration, be withdrawn by means of a notification addressed to the Secretary General of the Council of Europe. Such withdrawal shall take effect immediately or at such later date as may be specified in the notification.

Article 13

1. Any State may, at the time of signature or when depositing its instrument of ratification, acceptance or approval, declare that it reserves the right to refuse extradition in respect of any offence mentioned in Article 1 which it considers to be a political offence, an offence connected with a political offence or an offence inspired by political motives, provided that it undertakes to take into due consideration, when evaluating the character of the offence, any particularly serious aspects of the offence, including:

(*a*)   that it created a collective danger to the life, physical integrity or liberty of persons; or

(*b*)   that it affected persons foreign to the motives behind it; or

(*c*)   that cruel or vicious means have been used in the commission of the offence.

2. Any State may wholly or partly withdraw a reservation it has made in accordance with the foregoing paragraph by means of a declaration addressed to the Secretary General of the Council of Europe which shall become effective as from the date of its receipt.

3. A State which has made a reservation in accordance with paragraph 1 of this Article may not claim the application of Article 1 by any other State; it may, however, if its reservation is partial or conditional, claim the application of that Article in so far as it has itself accepted it.

Article 14

Any Contracting State may denounce this Convention by means of a written notification addressed to the Secretary General of the Council of Europe. Any such denunciation shall take effect immediately or at such later date as may be specified in the notification.

Article 15

This Convention ceases to have effect in respect of any Contracting State which withdraws from or ceases to be a member of the Council of Europe.

Article 16

The Secretary General of the Council of Europe shall notify the member States of the Council of:

(*a*)   any signature;

(*b*)   any deposit of an instrument of ratification, acceptance or approval;

(*c*)   any date of entry into force of this Convention in accordance with Article 11 thereof;

(*d*)   any declaration or notification received in pursuance of the provisions of Article 12;

(*e*)   any reservation made in pursuance of the provisions of Article 13, paragraph 1;

(*f*)   the withdrawal of any reservation effected in pursuance of the provisions of Article 13, paragraph 2;

(*g*)   any notification received in pursuance of Article 14 and the date on which denunciation takes effect;

(*h*)   any cessation of the effects of the Convention pursuant to Article 15.

IN WITNESS WHEREOF, the undersigned, being duly authorised thereto, have signed this Convention.

DONE at Strasbourg, this 27th day of January 1977, in English and in French, both texts being equally authoritative, in a single copy which shall remain deposited in the archives of the Council of Europe. The Secretary General of the Council of Europe shall transmit certified copies to each of the signatory States.

---

15. SAARC Regional Convention on Suppression of Terrorism

Signed at Kathmandu on 4 November 1987
In force on 22 August 1988
Depositary: Secretary-General of the South Asian Association for Regional Cooperation

The member States of the South Asian Association for Regional Cooperation (SAARC)

MINDFUL of the principles of cooperation enshrined in the SAARC Charter;

RECALLING that at the Dhaka Summit on December 7-8, 1985, the Heads of State or Government of the member States of the SAARC recognised the seriousness of the problem of terrorism as it affects the security and stability of the region;

ALSO RECALLING the Bangalore Summit Declaration of 17 November 1986, in which the Heads of State or Government of SAARC agreed that cooperation among SAARC States was vital if terrorism was to be prevented and eliminated from the region; unequivocally condemned all acts, methods and practices of terrorism as criminal and deplored their impact on life and property, socio-economic development, political stability, regional and international peace and cooperation; and recognised the importance of the principles laid down in UN Resolution 2625 (XXV) which among others required that each State should refrain from organising, instigating, assisting or participating in acts of civil strife or terrorist acts in another State or acquiescing in organised activities within its territory directed towards the commission of such acts;

AWARE of the danger posed by the spread of terrorism and its harmful effect on peace, cooperation, friendship and good neighbourly relations and which could also jeopardise the sovereignty and territorial integrity of States;

HAVE RESOLVED to take effective measures to ensure that perpetrators of terroristic acts do not escape prosecution and punishment by providing for their extradition or prosecution, and to this end,

HAVE AGREED as follows:

Article I

Subject to the overall requirements of the law of extradition, conduct constituting any of the following offences, according to the law of the Contracting State, shall be regarded as terroristic and for the purpose of extradition shall not be regarded as a political offence or as an offence connected with a political offence or as an offence inspired by political motives:

(*a*) An offence within the scope of the Convention for the Suppression of Unlawful Seizure of Aircraft, signed at The Hague on December 16, 1970;

(*b*) An offence within the scope of the Convention for the Suppression of Unlawful Acts against the Safety of Civil Aviation, signed at Montreal on September 23, 1971;

(*c*) An offence within the scope of the Convention on the Prevention and Punishment of Crimes against Internationally Protected Persons, including Diplomatic Agents, signed at New York on December 14, 1973;

(*d*) An offence within the scope of any Convention to which the SAARC member States concerned are parties and which obliges the parties to prosecute or grant extradition;

(*e*) Murder, manslaughter, assault causing bodily harm, kidnapping, hostage-taking and offences relating to firearms, weapons, explosives and dangerous substances when used as a means to perpetrate indiscriminate violence involving death or serious bodily injury to persons or serious damage to property;

(*f*) An attempt or conspiracy to commit an offence described in subparagraphs (*a*) to (*e*), aiding, abetting or counselling the commission of such an offence or participating as an accomplice in the offences so described.

Article II

For the purpose of extradition between the SAARC member States, any two or more Contracting States may, by agreement, decide to include any other serious offence involving violence, which shall not be regarded as a political offence or an offence connected with a political offence or an offence inspired by political motives.

Article III

1. The provisions of all extradition treaties and arrangements applicable between Contracting States are hereby amended as between Contracting States to the extent that they are incompatible with this Convention.

2. For the purpose of this Convention and to the extent that any offence referred to in Article I or agreed to in terms of Article II is not listed as an extraditable offence in any extradition treaty existing between Contracting States, it shall be deemed to be included as such therein.

3. Contracting States undertake to include these offences as extraditable offences in any future extradition treaty to be concluded between them.

4. If a Contracting State which makes extradition conditional on the existence of a treaty receives a request for extradition from another Contracting State with which it has no extradition treaty, the requested State may, at its option, consider this Convention as the basis for extradition in respect of the offences set forth in Article I or agreed to in terms of Article II. Extradition shall be subject to the law of the requested State.

5. Contracting States which do not make extradition conditional on the existence of a treaty, shall recognise the offences set forth in Article I or agreed to in terms of Article II as extraditable offences between themselves, subject to the law of the requested State.

Article IV

A Contracting State in whose territory a person suspected of having committed an offence referred to in Article I or agreed to in terms of Article II is found and which has received a request for extradition from another Contracting State, shall, if it does not extradite that person, submit the case without exception and without delay, to its competent authorities, so that prosecution may be considered. These authorities shall take their decisions in the same manner as in the case of any offence of a serious nature under the law of that State.

Article V

For the purpose of Article IV, each Contracting State may take such measures as it deems appropriate, consistent with its national laws, subject to reciprocity, to exercise its jurisdiction in the case of an offence under Article I or agreed to in terms of Article II.

Article VI

A Contracting State in whose territory an alleged offender is found, shall, upon receiving a request for extradition from another Contracting State, take appropriate measures, subject to its national laws, so as to ensure his presence for purposes of extradition or prosecution. Such measures shall immediately be notified to the requesting State.

Article VII

Contracting States shall not be obliged to extradite, if it appears to the requested State that by reason of the trivial nature of the case or by reason of the request for the surrender or return of a fugitive offender not being made in good faith or in the interests of justice or for any other reason it is unjust or inexpedient to surrender or return the fugitive offender.

Article VIII

1. Contracting States shall, subject to their national laws, afford one another the greatest measure of mutual assistance in connection with proceedings brought in respect of the offences referred to in Article I or agreed to in terms of Article II, including the supply of all evidence at their disposal necessary for the proceedings.

2. Contracting States shall cooperate among themselves, to the extent permitted by their national laws, through consultations between appropriate agencies, exchange of information, intelligence and expertise and such other cooperative measures as may be appropriate, with a view to preventing terroristic activities through precautionary measures.

Article IX

1. The Convention shall be open for signature by the member States of SAARC at the SAARC Secretariat in Kathmandu.

2. It shall be subject to ratification. Instruments of ratification shall be deposited with the Secretary-General of SAARC.

Article X

This Convention shall enter into force on the fifteenth day following the date of the deposit of the seventh instrument of ratification with the Secretary-General of SAARC.

Article XI

The Secretary-General of SAARC shall be the depositary of this Convention and shall notify member States of signatures to this Convention and all deposits of instruments of ratification. The Secretary-General shall transmit certified copies of such instruments to each member State. The Secretary-General shall also inform member States of the date on which this Convention will have entered into force in accordance with Article X.

IN WITNESS WHEREOF the undersigned, being duly authorised thereto by their respective Governments, have signed this Convention.

DONE at Kathmandu on this fourth day of November one thousand nine hundred and eighty-seven, in eight originals, in the English language, all texts being equally authentic.

In the name of Allah, the Beneficent and Merciful

16. The Arab Convention on the Suppression of Terrorism[1]

Signed at Cairo on 22 April 1998
Entry into force in accordance with Article 40
Depositary: General Secretariat of the League of Arab States

PREAMBLE

The Arab States signatory hereto,

DESIRING to promote mutual cooperation in the suppression of terrorist offences, which pose a threat to the security and stability of the Arab Nation and endanger its vital interests,

BEING COMMITTED to the highest moral and religious principles and, in particular, to the tenets of the Islamic Sharia, as well as to the humanitarian heritage of an Arab Nation that rejects all forms of violence and terrorism and advocates the protection of human rights, with which precepts the principles of international law conform, based as they are on cooperation among peoples in the promotion of peace,

BEING FURTHER COMMITTED to the Pact of the League of Arab States, the Charter of the United Nations and all the other international covenants and instruments to which the Contracting States to this Convention are parties,

AFFIRMING the right of peoples to combat foreign occupation and aggression by whatever means, including armed struggle, in order to liberate their territories and secure their right to self-determination and independence and to do so in such a manner as to preserve the territorial

---

[1] Translation from the Arabic original provided by the United Nations Secretariat.

integrity of each Arab country, the foregoing being in accordance with the purposes and principles of the Charter of the United Nations and with the Organization's resolutions,

HAVE AGREED to conclude this Convention and to invite any Arab State that did not participate in its conclusion to accede hereto.

PART ONE
DEFINITIONS AND GENERAL PROVISIONS

Article 1

Each of the following terms shall be understood in the light of the definition given:

1.   *Contracting State*

Any member State of the League of Arab States that has ratified this Convention and that has deposited its instruments of ratification with the General Secretariat of the League.

2.   *Terrorism*

Any act or threat of violence, whatever its motives or purposes, that occurs for the advancement of an individual or collective criminal agenda, causing terror among people, causing fear by harming them, or placing their lives, liberty or security in danger, or aiming to cause damage to the environment or to public or private installations or property or to occupy or seize them, or aiming to jeopardize a national resource.

3.   *Terrorist offence*

Any offence or attempted offence committed in furtherance of a terrorist objective in any of the Contracting States, or against their nationals, property or interests, that is punishable by their domestic law. The offences stipulated in the following conventions, except where conventions have not been ratified by Contracting States or where offences have been excluded by their legislation, shall also be regarded as terrorist offences:

(a)   The Tokyo Convention on Offences and Certain Other Acts Committed on Board Aircraft, of 14 September 1963;

(b)   The Hague Convention for the Suppression of Unlawful Seizure of Aircraft, of 16 December 1970;

(c)   The Montreal Convention for the Suppression of Unlawful Acts against the Safety of Civil Aviation, of 23 September 1971, and the Protocol thereto of 10 May 1984;

(d)   The Convention on the Prevention and Punishment of Crimes against Internationally Protected Persons, including Diplomatic Agents, of 14 December 1973;

(e)   The International Convention against the Taking of Hostages, of 17 December 1979;

(f)   The provisions of the United Nations Convention on the Law of the Sea, of 1982, relating to piracy on the high seas.

Article 2

(a) All cases of struggle by whatever means, including armed struggle, against foreign occupation and aggression for liberation and self-determination, in accordance with the principles of international law, shall not be regarded as an offence. This provision shall not apply to any act prejudicing the territorial integrity of any Arab State.

(b) None of the terrorist offences indicated in the preceding Article shall be regarded as a political offence. In the application of this Convention, none of the following offences shall be regarded as a political offence, even if committed for political motives:

(i)   Attacks on the kings, heads of State or rulers of the Contracting States or on their spouses and families;

(ii)   Attacks on crown princes, vice-presidents, prime ministers or ministers in any of the Contracting States;

(iii)   Attacks on persons enjoying diplomatic immunity, including ambassadors and diplomats serving in or accredited to the Contracting States;

(iv)   Premeditated murder or theft accompanied by the use of force directed against individuals, the authorities or means of transport and communications;

(v)   Acts of sabotage and destruction of public property and property assigned to a public service, even if owned by another Contracting State;

(vi)   The manufacture, illicit trade in or possession of weapons, munitions or explosives, or other items that may be used to commit terrorist offences.

PART TWO
PRINCIPLES OF ARAB COOPERATION FOR THE SUPPRESSION OF
TERRORISM

CHAPTER I
THE SECURITY FIELD

SECTION A
MEASURES FOR THE PREVENTION AND SUPPRESSION OF
TERRORIST OFFENCES

Article 3

Contracting States undertake not to organize, finance or commit terrorist acts or to be accessories thereto in any manner whatsoever. In their commitment to the prevention and suppression of terrorist offences in accordance with their domestic laws and procedures, they shall endeavour:

I.   Preventive measures

1.   To prevent the use of their territories as a base for planning, organizing, executing, attempting or taking part in terrorist

155

crimes in any manner whatsoever. This includes the prevention of terrorists' infiltration into, or residence in, their territories either as individuals or groups, receiving or giving refuge to them, training, arming, financing, or providing any facilitation to them;

2.   To cooperate and coordinate action among Contracting States, particularly neighbouring countries suffering from similar or common terrorist offences;

3.   To develop and strengthen systems for the detection of the movement, importation, exportation, stockpiling and use of weapons, munitions and explosives and of other means of aggression, murder and destruction as well as procedures for monitoring their passage through customs and across borders in order to prevent their transfer from one Contracting State to another or to third-party States other than for lawful purposes;

4.   To develop and strengthen systems concerned with surveillance procedures and the securing of borders and points of entry overland and by air in order to prevent illicit entry thereby;

5.   To strengthen mechanisms for the security and protection of eminent persons, vital installations and means of public transportation;

6.   To enhance the protection, security and safety of diplomatic and consular persons and missions and international and regional organizations accredited to Contracting States, in accordance with the relevant international agreements which govern this subject;

7.   To reinforce security-related information activities and to coordinate them with those of each State in accordance with its information policy, with a view to exposing the objectives of terrorist groups and organizations, thwarting their schemes and demonstrating the danger they pose to security and stability;

8.   To establish, in each Contracting State, a database for the

accumulation and analysis of information relating to terrorist elements, groups, movements and organizations and for the monitoring of developments with respect to the terrorist phenomenon and of successful experiences in counterterrorism; and to keep such information up to date and make it available to the competent authorities of Contracting States, within the limits established by the domestic laws and procedures of each State.

II.   Measures of suppression

1.   To arrest the perpetrators of terrorist offences and to prosecute them in accordance with national law or extradite them in accordance with the provisions of this Convention or of any bilateral treaty between the requesting State and the requested State;

2.   To provide effective protection for those working in the criminal justice field;

3.   To provide effective protection for sources of information concerning terrorist offences and for witnesses thereto;

4.   To extend necessary assistance to victims of terrorism;

5.   To establish effective cooperation between the relevant agencies and the public in countering terrorism by, *inter alia*, establishing appropriate guarantees and incentives to encourage the reporting of terrorist acts, the provision of information to assist in their investigation, and cooperation in the arrest of perpetrators.

SECTION B
ARAB COOPERATION FOR THE PREVENTION AND SUPPRESSION
OF TERRORIST OFFENCES

Article 4

Contracting States shall cooperate for the prevention and suppression of terrorist offences, in accordance with the domestic laws and regulations of each State, as set forth hereunder.

I.   *Exchange of information*

1.   Contracting States shall undertake to promote the exchange of information between and among them concerning:

   (*a*)   The activities and crimes of terrorist groups and of their leaders and members; their headquarters and training; the means and sources by which they are funded and armed; the types of weapons, munitions and explosives used by them; and other means of aggression, murder and destruction;

   (*b*)   The means of communication and propaganda used by terrorist groups; their modus operandi ; the movements of their leaders and members; and the travel documents that they use.

2.   Each Contracting State shall undertake to notify any other Contracting State in an expeditious manner of the information it has concerning any terrorist offence that takes place in its territory and is intended to harm the interests of that State or of its nationals and to include in such notification statements concerning the circumstances surrounding the offence, those who committed it, its victims, the losses occasioned by it and the devices and methods used in its perpetration, to the extent compatible with the requirements of the investigation and inquiry.

3.   Contracting States shall undertake to cooperate with each other in the exchange of information for the suppression of terrorist offences and promptly to notify other Contracting States of all the information or data in their possession that may prevent the occurrence of terrorist offences in their territory, against their nationals or residents or against their interests.

4.   Each Contracting State shall undertake to furnish any other Contracting State with any information or data in its possession that may:

(*a*)   Assist in the arrest of a person or persons accused of committing a terrorist offence against the interests of that State or of being implicated in such an offence whether by aiding and abetting, collusion or incitement;

(*b*)   Lead to the seizure of any weapons, munitions or explosives or any devices or funds used or intended for use to commit a terrorist offence.

5.   Contracting States shall undertake to maintain the confidentiality of the information that they exchange among themselves and not to furnish it to any State that is not a Contracting State or any other party without the prior consent of the State that was the source of the information.

II.   Investigations

Contracting States shall undertake to promote cooperation among themselves and to provide assistance with respect to measures for the investigation and arrest of fugitives suspected or convicted of terrorist offences in accordance with the laws and regulations of each State.

III.   Exchange of expertise

1.   Contracting States shall cooperate in the conduct and exchange of research studies for the suppression of terrorist offences and shall exchange expertise in the counterterrorism field.

2.   Contracting States shall cooperate, within the limits of their resources, in providing all possible technical assistance for the formulation of programmes or the holding of joint training courses or training courses intended for one State or for a group of Contracting States, as required, for the benefit of those working in counterterrorism with the aim of developing their scientific and practical abilities and enhancing their performance.

CHAPTER II
THE JUDICIAL FIELD

SECTION A
EXTRADITION OF OFFENDERS

Article 5

Contracting States shall undertake to extradite those indicted for or convicted of terrorist offences whose extradition is requested by any of these States in accordance with the rules and conditions stipulated in this Convention.

Article 6

Extradition shall not be permissible in any of the following circumstances:

(*a*)   If the offence for which extradition is requested is regarded under the laws in force in the requested State as an offence of a political nature;

(*b*)   If the offence for which extradition is requested relates solely to a dereliction of military duties;

(*c*)   If the offence for which extradition is requested was committed in the territory of the requested Contracting State, except where the offence has harmed the interests of the requesting State and its laws provide for the prosecution and punishment for such offences and where the requested State has not initiated any investigation or prosecution;

(*d*)   If a final judgement having the force of *res judicata* has been rendered in respect of the offence in the requested Contracting State or in a third Contracting State;

(*e*)   If, on delivery of the request for extradition, proceedings have been terminated or punishment has, under the law of the requesting State, lapsed because of the passage of time;

(*f*)   If the offence was committed outside the territory of the requesting State by a person who is not a national of that State and the law of the requested State does not allow prosecution for the same category of offence when committed outside its territory by such a person;

(*g*)   If the requesting State has granted amnesty to perpetrators of offences that include the offence in question;

(*h*)   If the legal system of the requested State does not allow it to extradite its nationals. In this case, the requested State shall prosecute any such persons who commit in any of the other Contracting States a terrorist offence that is punishable in both States by deprivation of liberty for a period of at least one year or more. The nationality of the person whose extradition is sought shall be determined as at the date on which the offence in question was committed, and use shall be made in this regard of the investigation conducted by the requesting State.

Article 7

Should the person whose extradition is sought be under investigation, on trial or already convicted for another offence in the requested State, his extradition shall be deferred until such time as the investigation is concluded, the trial is completed or the sentence is imposed. The requested State may nevertheless extradite him on an interim basis for questioning or trial provided that he is returned to that State before serving the sentence imposed on him in the requesting State.

Article 8

For purposes of the extradition of offenders under this Convention, no account shall be taken of any difference there may be in the domestic legislation of Contracting States in the legal designation of the offence as a felony or a misdemeanour or in the penalty assigned to it, provided that it is punishable under the laws of both States by deprivation of liberty for a period of at least one year or more.

SECTION B
JUDICIAL DELEGATION

Article 9

Each Contracting State may request any other Contracting State to undertake in its territory and on its behalf any judicial procedure relating to an action arising out of a terrorist offence and, in particular:

(*a*)   To hear the testimony of witnesses and take depositions as evidence;

(*b*)   To effect service of judicial documents;

(*c*)   To execute searches and seizures;

(*d*)   To examine and inspect evidence;

(*e*)   To obtain relevant documents and records or certified copies thereof.

Article 10

Each of the Contracting States shall undertake to implement judicial delegations relating to terrorist offences, but such assistance may be refused in either of the two following cases:

(*a*)   Where the request relates to an offence that is subject to investigation or prosecution in the requested State;

(*b*)   Where granting the request might be prejudicial to the sovereignty, security or public order of the requested State.

Article 11

The request for judicial delegation shall be granted promptly in accordance with the provisions of the domestic law of the requested State. The latter may postpone the execution of the request until such time as any ongoing investigation or prosecution involving the same matter is completed or any compelling reasons for postponement cease to exist, provided that the requesting State is notified of such postponement.

Article 12

(*a*) A measure that is undertaken by means of a judicial delegation, in accordance with the provisions of this Convention, shall have the same legal effect as if it had been taken by the competent authority of the requesting State.

(*b*) The result of implementing the judicial delegation may be used only for the purpose for which the delegation is issued.

SECTION C
JUDICIAL COOPERATION

Article 13

Each Contracting State shall provide the other States with all possible and necessary assistance for investigations or prosecutions relating to terrorist offences.

Article 14

(*a*) Where one of the Contracting States has jurisdiction to prosecute a person suspected of a terrorist offence, it may request the State in which the suspect is present to take proceedings against him for that offence, subject to the agreement of that State and provided that the offence is punishable in the prosecuting State by deprivation of liberty for a period of at least one year or more. The requesting State shall, in this event, provide the requested State with all the investigation documents and evidence relating to the offence.

(*b*) The investigation or prosecution shall be conducted on the basis of the charge or charges made by the requesting State against the suspect, in accordance with the provisions and procedures of the law of the prosecuting State.

Article 15

The submission by the requesting State of a request for prosecution in accordance with paragraph (*a*) of the preceding Article shall entail the suspension of the measures taken by it to pursue, investigate and prosecute the suspect whose prosecution is being requested, with the exception of those required for the purposes of the judicial cooperation and assistance, or the judicial delegation, sought by the State requested to conduct the prosecution.

Article 16

(*a*) The measures taken in either the requesting State or that in which the prosecution takes place shall be subject to the law of the State in which they are taken and they shall have the force accorded to them by that law.

(*b*) The requesting State may try or retry a person whose prosecution it has requested only if the requested State declines to prosecute him.

(*c*) The State requested to take proceedings shall in all cases undertake to notify the requesting State of what action it has taken with regard to the request and of the outcome of the investigation or prosecution.

Article 17

The State requested to take proceedings may take all the measures and steps established by its law with respect to the accused both before the request to take proceedings reaches it and subsequently.

Article 18

The transfer of competence for prosecution shall not prejudice the rights of the victim of the offence, who reserves the right to approach the courts of the requesting State or the prosecuting State with a view to claiming his civil-law rights as a result of the offence.

SECTION D
SEIZURE OF ASSETS AND PROCEEDS DERIVED FROM THE OFFENCE

Article 19

(*a*) If it is decided to extradite the requested person, any Contracting State shall undertake to seize and hand over to the requesting State the property used and proceeds derived from or relating to the terrorist offence, whether in the possession of the person whose extradition is sought or of a third party.

(*b*) Once it has been established that they relate to the terrorist offence, the items indicated in the preceding paragraph shall be surrendered even if the person to be extradited is not handed over because he has absconded or died or for any other reason.

(*c*) The provisions of the two preceding paragraphs shall be without prejudice to the rights of any Contracting State or of *bona fide* third parties in the property or proceeds in question.

Article 20

The State requested to hand over property and proceeds may take all the precautionary measures necessary to discharge its obligation to hand them over. It may also retain such property or proceeds on a temporary basis if they are required for pending criminal proceedings or may, for the same reason, hand them over to the requesting State on condition that they are returned.

SECTION E
EXCHANGE OF EVIDENCE

Article 21

Contracting States shall undertake to have the evidence of any terrorist offence committed in their territory against another Contracting State examined by their competent agencies, and they may seek the assistance of any other Contracting State in doing so. They shall take the necessary measures to preserve such evidence and ensure its legal validity. They alone shall have the right, when so requested, to communicate the outcome of the examination to the State against whose interests the offence was committed, and the Contracting State or States whose assistance is sought shall not pass this information to any third party.

PART THREE
MECHANISMS FOR IMPLEMENTING COOPERATION

CHAPTER I
EXTRADITION PROCEDURES

Article 22

Requests for extradition shall be made between the competent authorities in the Contracting States directly, through their ministries of justice or the equivalent or through the diplomatic channel.

Article 23

The request for extradition shall be made in writing and shall be accompanied by the following:

(*a*)   The original or an authenticated copy of the indictment or detention order or any other documents having the same effect and issued in accordance with the procedure laid down in the law of the requesting State;

(*b*)   A statement of the offences for which extradition is requested, showing the time and place of their commission, their legal designation and a reference to the legal provisions applicable thereto, together with a copy of the relevant provisions;

(*c*)   As accurate a description as possible of the person whose extradition is sought, together with any other information that may serve to establish his identity and nationality.

Article 24

1. The judicial authorities in the requesting State may apply to the requested State by any of the means of written communication for the provisional detention of the person being sought pending the presentation of the request for extradition.

2. In this case, the State from which extradition is requested may detain the person being sought on a provisional basis. If the request for extradition is not presented together with the necessary documents specified in the preceding Article, the person whose extradition is being sought may not be detained for more than 30 days from the date of his arrest.

Article 25

The requesting State shall submit a request accompanied by the documents specified in Article 23 of this Convention. If the requested State determines that the request is in order, its competent authorities shall grant the request in accordance with its own law and its decision shall be promptly communicated to the requesting State.

Article 26

1. In all of the cases stipulated in the two preceding Articles, the period of provisional detention shall not exceed 60 days from the date of arrest.

2. During the period specified in the preceding paragraph, the possibility of provisional release is not excluded provided that the State from which extradition is requested takes any measures it considers necessary to prevent the escape of the person sought.

3. Such release shall not prevent the rearrest of the person concerned or his extradition if a request for extradition is received subsequently.

Article 27

Should the requested State consider that it requires supplementary information in order to ascertain whether the conditions stipulated in this Chapter have been met, it shall notify the requesting State accordingly and a date for the provision of such information shall be established.

Article 28

Should the requested State receive several requests for extradition from different States, either for the same offence or for different offences, it shall make its decision having regard to all the circumstances and, in particular, the possibility of subsequent extradition, the respective dates of when the requests were received, the relative seriousness of the offences and the place where the offences were committed.

CHAPTER II
PROCEDURES FOR JUDICIAL DELEGATION

Article 29

Requests relating to judicial delegations shall contain the following information:

(*a*)   The authority presenting the request;

(*b*)   The subject of and reason for the request;

(*c*)   An exact statement, to the extent possible, of the identity and nationality of the person concerned;

(*d*)   A description of the offence in connection with which the request for a judicial delegation is being made, its legal designation, the penalty established for its commission, and as much information as possible on the circumstances so as to facilitate the proper functioning of the judicial delegation.

Article 30

1. The request for a judicial delegation shall be addressed by the Ministry of Justice of the requesting State to the Ministry of Justice of the requested State and shall be returned through the same channel.

2. In case of urgency, the request for a judicial delegation shall be addressed by the judicial authorities of the requesting State directly to the judicial authorities of the requested State, and a copy of the request shall be sent at the same time to the Ministry of Justice of the requested State. The request, accompanied by the documents relating to its implementation, shall be returned through the channel stipulated in the preceding paragraph.

3. The request for a judicial delegation may be sent by the judicial authorities directly to the competent authority in the requested State, and replies may be forwarded directly through this authority.

Article 31

Requests for judicial delegations and their accompanying documents must be signed and must bear the seal of the competent authority or be authenticated by it. Such documents shall be exempt from all formalities that may be required by the legislation of the requested State.

Article 32

Should an authority that receives a request for a judicial delegation not have the competence to deal with the request, it shall automatically refer the request to the competent authority in its State. In the event the request has been sent directly, it shall notify the requesting State in the same manner.

Article 33

Every refusal of a request for a judicial delegation must be accompanied by a statement of the grounds for such refusal.

CHAPTER III
MEASURES FOR THE PROTECTION OF WITNESSES AND EXPERTS

Article 34

If, in the estimation of a requesting State, the appearance of a witness or expert before its judicial authority is of particular importance, it shall indicate this fact in its request. The request or summons to appear shall indicate the approximate amount of the allowances and the travel and subsistence expenses and shall include an undertaking to pay them. The requested State shall invite the witness or expert to appear and shall inform the requesting State of the response.

Article 35

1. A witness or an expert who does not comply with a summons to appear shall not be subject to any penalty or coercive measure, notwithstanding any contrary statement in the summons.

2. Where a witness or an expert travels to the territory of the requesting State of his own accord, he should be summoned to appear in accordance with the provisions of the domestic legislation of that State.

Article 36

1. A witness or an expert shall not be prosecuted, detained or subjected to any restrictions on his personal liberty in the territory of the requesting State in respect of any acts or convictions that preceded the person's departure from the requested State, regardless of his nationality, as long as his appearance before the judicial authorities of that State is in response to a summons.

2. No witness or expert, regardless of his nationality, who appears before the judicial authorities of a requesting State in response to a summons may be prosecuted, detained or subjected to any restrictions on his personal liberty in the territory of that State in respect of any acts or convictions not specified in the summons and that preceded the person's departure from the territory of the requested State.

3. The immunity stipulated in this Article shall lapse if the witness or expert sought, being free to leave, remains in the territory of the requesting State for a period of 30 consecutive days after his presence is no longer required by the judicial authorities or, having left the territory of the requesting State, has voluntarily returned.

Article 37

1. The requesting State shall take all necessary measures to protect witnesses and experts from any publicity that might endanger them, their families or their property as a result of their provision of testimony or expertise and shall, in particular, guarantee confidentiality with respect to:

(*a*)   The date, place and means of their arrival in the requesting State;

(*b*)   Their place of residence, their movements and the places they frequent;

(*c*)   Their testimony and the information they provide before the competent judicial authorities.

2. The requesting State shall undertake to provide the necessary protection for the security of witnesses and experts and of members of their families that is required by their situation, the circumstances of the case in connection with which they are sought and the types of risks that can be anticipated.

Article 38

1. Where a witness or expert whose appearance is sought by a requesting State is in custody in the requested State, he may be temporarily transferred to the location of the hearing where he is requested to provide his testimony under conditions and at times to be determined by the requested State. Such transfer may be refused if:

(*a*)   The witness or expert in custody objects;

(*b*)   His presence is required for criminal proceedings in the territory

171

of the requested State;

(*c*)   His transfer would prolong the term of his detention;

(*d*)   There are considerations militating against his transfer.

2. The witness or expert thus transferred shall continue to be held in custody in the territory of the requesting State until such time as he is returned to the requested State unless the latter State requests that he be released.

PART FOUR
FINAL PROVISIONS

Article 39

This Convention is subject to ratification, acceptance or approval by the signatory States, and instruments of ratification, acceptance or approval shall be deposited with the General Secretariat of the League of Arab States within 30 days of the date of such ratification, acceptance or approval. The General Secretariat shall notify member States of the deposit of each such instrument and of its date.

Article 40

1. This Convention shall enter into force on the thirtieth day after the date as of which instruments of ratification, acceptance or approval have been deposited by seven Arab States.

2. This Convention shall enter into force for any other Arab State only after the instrument of ratification, acceptance or approval has been deposited and 30 days have elapsed from the date of that deposit.

Article 41

No Contracting State may make any reservation that explicitly or implicitly violates the provisions of this Convention or is incompatible with its objectives.

Article 42

A Contracting State may denounce this Convention only by written request addressed to the Secretary-General of the League of Arab States.

Denunciation shall take effect six months from the date the request is addressed to the Secretary-General of the League of Arab States.

The provisions of this Convention shall remain in force in respect of requests submitted before this period expires.

DONE at Cairo, this twenty-second day of April 1998, in a single copy, which shall be deposited with the General Secretariat of the League of Arab States. A certified copy shall be kept at the General Secretariat of the Council of Arab Ministers of the Interior, and certified copies shall be transmitted to each of the parties that are signatories to this Convention or that accede hereto.

IN WITNESS WHEREOF, the Arab Ministers of the Interior and Ministers of Justice have signed this Convention on behalf of their respective States.

173

17. Treaty on Cooperation among the States Members of the Commonwealth of Independent States in Combating Terrorism, 1999[2]

Done at Minsk on 4 June 1999
Entry into force in accordance with Article 22
Depositary: Executive Committee of the Commonwealth of Independent States

The States parties to this Treaty, in the person of their Governments, hereinafter referred to as the Parties,

Aware of the danger posed by acts of terrorism,

Bearing in mind the instruments adopted within the United Nations and the Commonwealth of Independent States, as well as other international instruments, relating to combating the various manifestations of terrorism,

Wishing to render one another the broadest possible assistance in increasing the effectiveness of cooperation in this field,

Have agreed as follows:

Article 1

For purposes of this Treaty, the terms used in it mean:

"Terrorism" - an illegal act punishable under criminal law committed for the purpose of undermining public safety, influencing decision-making by the authorities or terrorizing the population, and taking the form of:

---

[2] Translation from the Russian original provided by the United Nations Secretariat, and approved by the Executive Committee of the Commonwealth of Independent States.

Violence or the threat of violence against natural or juridical persons;

Destroying (damaging) or threatening to destroy (damage) property and other material objects so as to endanger people's lives;

Causing substantial harm to property or the occurrence of other consequences dangerous to society;

Threatening the life of a statesman or public figure for the purpose of putting an end to his State or other public activity or in revenge for such activity;

Attacking a representative of a foreign State or an internationally protected staff member of an international organization, as well as the business premises or vehicles of internationally protected persons;

Other acts classified as terrorist under the national legislation of the Parties or under universally recognized international legal instruments aimed at combating terrorism;

"Technological terrorism" - the use or threat of the use of nuclear, radiological, chemical or bacteriological (biological) weapons or their components, pathogenic micro-organisms, radioactive substances or other substances harmful to human health, including the seizure, putting out of operation or destruction of nuclear, chemical or other facilities posing an increased technological and environmental danger and the utility systems of towns and other inhabited localities, if these acts are committed for the purpose of undermining public safety, terrorizing the population or influencing the decisions of the authorities in order to achieve political, mercenary or any other ends, as well as attempts to commit one of the crimes listed above for the same purposes and leading, financing or acting as the instigator, accessory or accomplice of a person who commits or attempts to commit such a crime;

"Facilities posing an increased technological and environmental danger" - enterprises, installations, plant and other facilities whose

175

inoperability may lead to loss of human life, the impairment of human health, pollution of the environment or destabilization of the situation in a given region or a given State as a whole;

"Special anti-terrorist units" - groups of specialists formed by the Parties in accordance with their national legislation to combat acts of terrorism;

"Special items and supplies" - materials, machinery and vehicles, personal equipment for members of special anti-terrorist units including weapons and ammunition, and special items and equipment.

Article 2

The Parties shall cooperate in preventing, uncovering, halting and investigating acts of terrorism in accordance with this Treaty, their national legislation and their international obligations.

Article 3

1. Each of the Parties shall, on signing this Treaty or carrying out the domestic procedures required for its entry into force, indicate its competent authorities responsible for implementing the provisions of this Treaty.

The Parties shall immediately notify the depositary of any changes with regard to their competent authority.

2. In implementing the provisions of this Treaty, the competent authorities of the Parties shall maintain direct relations with one another.

Article 4

1. In cooperating in combating acts of terrorism, including in relation to the extradition of persons committing them, the Parties shall not regard the acts involved as other than criminal.

2. The nationality of a person accused of an act of terrorism shall be deemed to be his nationality at the time of commission of the act.

Article 5

1. The competent authorities of the Party shall, in accordance with this Treaty, other international agreements and national legislation, cooperate and assist one another by:

(*a*)   Exchanging information;

(*b*)   Responding to enquiries regarding the conduct of investigations;

(*c*)   Developing and adopting agreed measures for preventing, uncovering, halting or investigating acts of terrorism, and informing one another about such measures;

(*d*)   Adopting measures to prevent and halt preparations in their territory for the commission of acts of terrorism in the territory of another Party;

(*e*)   Assisting in assessing the condition of the system for physical protection of facilities posing an increased technological and environmental danger, and developing and implementing measures to improve that system;

(*f*)   Exchanging legislative texts and materials on the practice with respect to their application;

(*g*)   Sending, by agreement between interested Parties, special anti-terrorist units to render practical assistance in halting acts of terrorism and combating their consequences;

(*h*)   Exchanging experience on the prevention and combating of terrorist acts, including the holding of training courses, seminars, consultations and workshops;

(*i*)   Training and further specialized training of personnel;

(*j*)   Joint financing, by agreement between Parties, and conduct of research and development work on systems for and means of physically protecting facilities posing an increased technological and environmental danger;

(*k*)   Implementation on a contractual basis of deliveries of special items, technology and equipment for anti-terrorist activity.

2. The procedure for sending and executing requests for extradition, for the provision of legal aid in criminal cases and for the institution of criminal proceedings shall be determined by the international agreements to which the Parties concerned are parties.

Article 6

The Parties shall, through joint consultations, jointly draw up recommendations for achieving concerted approaches to the legal regulation of issues relating to the prevention and combating of terrorist acts.

Article 7

1. Cooperation under this Treaty shall be conducted on the basis of requests by an interested Party for assistance to be rendered, or on the initiative of a Party which believes such assistance to be of interest to another Party.

2. The request for the rendering of assistance shall be made in writing. In urgent cases requests may be transmitted orally, but must be confirmed in writing not later than 72 hours thereafter, including through the use of technical text transmission facilities.

If doubt arises as to the genuineness or content of a request, additional confirmation may be requested.

Requests shall contain:

(*a*)   The name of the competent authority requesting assistance and of the authority requested; a statement of the substance of the matter; the purpose of and justification for the request; and a description of the nature of the assistance requested;

(*b*)   Any other information that may be useful for the proper fulfilment of the request.

3. A request for the rendering of assistance transmitted or confirmed in writing shall be signed by the head of the requesting competent authority or his deputy and shall be certified by the seal of the competent authority.

Article 8

1. The requested Party shall take all necessary measures to ensure the prompt and fullest possible fulfilment of the request.

The requesting Party shall be immediately notified of circumstances that prevent or will substantially delay the fulfilment of the request.

2. If the fulfilment of the request does not fall within the competence of the requested competent authority, it shall transmit the request to an authority of its State which is competent to fulfil it, and shall immediately so inform the requesting competent authority.

3. The requested Party shall be entitled to request additional information that is in its view needed for the proper fulfilment of the request.

4. In fulfilling a request, the legislation of the requested Party shall be applied; however, at the request of the requesting Party, its legislation may be applied if that does not contradict fundamental principles of the legislation of the requested Party or its international obligations.

5. If the requested Party considers that immediate fulfilment of the request may impede a criminal prosecution or other proceedings taking place on its territory, it may postpone fulfilment of the request or tie its fulfilment to compliance with conditions determined to be necessary following consultations with the requesting Party. If the requesting Party agrees that assistance shall be rendered to it on the proposed terms, it shall comply with those terms.

6. The requested Party shall at the request of the requesting Party take the necessary measures to ensure confidentiality of the fact that the request has been received, the content of the request and accompanying

179

documents, and the rendering of assistance.

If it is impossible to fulfil the request without maintaining confidentiality, the requested Party shall so inform the requesting Party, which shall decide whether the request should be fulfilled under those conditions.

7. The requested Party shall inform the requesting Party as soon as possible about the results of the fulfilment of the request.

Article 9

1. The rendering of assistance under this Treaty shall be denied in whole or in part if the requested Party believes that fulfilment of the request may impair its sovereignty, security, social order or other vital interests or is in contravention of its legislation or international obligations.

2. The rendering of assistance may be denied if the act in relation to which the request was made is not a crime under the legislation of the requested Party.

3. The requesting Party shall be notified in writing of a refusal to fulfil a request in whole or in part, with an indication of the reasons for refusal listed in paragraph 1 of this Article.

Article 10

1. Each Party shall ensure confidentiality of information and documents received from another Party if they are classified as restricted or the transmitting Party considers it undesirable that they should be made public. The level of security classification of such information and documents shall be determined by the transmitting Party.

2. Results of the fulfilment of a request obtained on the basis of this Treaty may not without the consent of the Party providing them be used for purposes other than those for which they were requested and provided.

3. Transmission to a third party of information obtained by one Party on the basis of this Treaty shall require the prior consent of the Party

providing the information.

Article 11

The competent authorities of the Parties shall exchange information on issues of mutual interest, including:

(*a*)   Materials distributed in the territory of their States containing information on terrorist threats, terrorist acts in the course of preparation or committed and the identified intentions of given persons, groups of persons or organizations to commit acts of terrorism;

(*b*)   Acts of terrorism in the course of preparation that are directed against heads of State, internationally protected persons, staff of diplomatic missions, consular institutions and international organizations of the Parties and participants in State visits and international and national political, sporting and other activities;

(*c*)   Instances of illegal circulation of nuclear materials, chemical, bacteriological (biological) weapons or their components, highly toxic chemicals and pathogenic micro-organisms;

(*d*)   Terrorist organizations, groups and individuals that present a threat to the State security of the Parties and the establishment of contacts between terrorist organizations, groups or individuals;

(*e*)   Illegal armed formations employing methods of terrorist activity, their structure, members, aims and objectives;

(*f*)   Ways, means and methods of terrorist action they have identified;

(*g*)   Supplies and equipment that may be provided by the Parties to one another to the extent of their ability;

(*h*)   Practice with respect to the legal and other regulatory settlement of issues related to the subject of this Treaty;

(*i*)   Identified and presumed channels for the financing and illegal delivery to the territory of their States of weapons and other means of committing terrorist acts;

(*j*)   Terrorist encroachments aimed at violating the sovereignty and territorial integrity of Parties;

Other issues of interest to the Parties.

Article 12

1. The Parties may, at the request or with the consent of the Party concerned, send representatives of their competent authorities, including special anti-terrorist units, to provide procedural, advisory or practical aid in accordance with this Treaty.

In such cases, the receiving Party shall notify the other Party in writing of the place and time of and procedure for crossing its State border and the nature of the problems to be dealt with, and shall promote and facilitate the necessary conditions for their effective solution, including unimpeded carriage of persons and special items and supplies and cost-free accommodation, food and use of the transport infrastructure of the receiving Party.

Any movement of a special anti-terrorist unit or of individual members of such a unit within the territory of the receiving Party shall be possible only with special permission from and under the control of the head of the competent authority of the receiving Party.

2. The procedure for the use of air, road, rail, river and maritime transport to provide aid shall be determined by the competent authorities of the Parties in agreement with the relevant ministries and departments of the receiving Party.

Article 13

1. For purposes of the effective and timely provision of aid, the Parties shall, when special anti-terrorist units cross the State border, ensure accelerated conduct of the formalities established by national legislation.

2. At the border crossing point, the commanding officer of a special anti-terrorist unit shall present the nominal role of members of the

group and list of special items and supplies certified by the competent authorities of the sending Party, together with an indication of the purposes of the Unit's arrival in the territory of the receiving Party, while all members of the group shall present their national passports and documents confirming that they belong to competent authorities for combating terrorism.

3. Special items and supplies shall be exempt from customs duties and payments and must be either used during the operation for the provision of aid or removed from the territory of the receiving Party upon its conclusion.

If special circumstances make it impossible to remove the special items and supplies, the competent authorities of the sending Party shall hand them over to the competent authorities of the receiving Party.

Article 14

The decision on the procedure for conducting special measures under this Treaty shall be taken by the competent authority of the receiving Party, taking into account the views of the commanding officer of the incoming anti-terrorist unit of the other Party. If these views are not taken into account, the commanding officer shall be entitled to refuse to participate in the conduct of the special measure.

Article 15

1. The receiving Party shall refrain from any claims against a Party providing aid, including with regard to compensation for damages arising out of death, bodily injury or any other harm caused to the lives, health and property of natural persons located in the territory of the receiving Party, and also to juridical persons and the receiving Party itself, if such harm was inflicted during the performance of activities associated with the implementation of this Treaty.

2. If a participant in the special anti-terrorist unit of the sending Party inflicts harm on some person or organization while performing activities associated with the implementation of this Treaty in the territory of the receiving Party, the receiving Party shall make compensation for

the harm in accordance with the provisions of national legislation which would be applied in the case of harm being inflicted by members of anti-terrorist units of the receiving Party in similar circumstances.

3. The procedure for repayment of expenses incurred by the sending Party, including expenses associated with the loss or complete or partial destruction of imported special items and supplies, shall be established by agreement between the Parties concerned.

4. If one of the Parties considers the damage caused by the actions of the special anti-terrorist unit to be disproportionate to the purposes of the operation, the differences of opinion that arise shall be settled at the bilateral level by the Parties concerned.

Article 16

For purposes of the implementation of this Treaty, the competent authorities of the Parties may where necessary hold consultations and working meetings.

Article 17

The Parties may, by mutual agreement and on the basis of separate agreements, conduct joint exercises of special anti-terrorist units and, on a reciprocal basis, organize training for representatives of another Party in their national anti-terrorist detachments.

Article 18

1. Materials, special items, technology and equipment received by the competent authorities of the Parties pursuant to this Agreement may be transferred to a third party only with the consent of and on the terms specified by the competent authority which provided such materials, special items, technology and equipment.

2. Information on the investigation methods of special anti-terrorist units and on the characteristics of special forces and of items and supplies used in providing aid under this Agreement may not be disclosed.

Article 19

The Parties concerned shall where necessary agree on the financial, organizational and technical and other conditions for the provision of assistance under this Agreement.

Article 20

1. This Treaty shall not limit the right of the Parties to conclude bilateral international agreements on issues which are the subject of this Treaty, and shall not affect the rights and obligations of Parties arising out of other international agreements to which they are parties.

2. The competent authorities of the Parties may conclude with one another agreements that regulate in more detail the procedure for implementation of this Treaty.

Article 21

Disputes arising out of the interpretation or application of this Treaty shall be resolved through consultations and negotiations between the Parties.

Article 22

This Treaty shall enter into force on the date of its signature, and for Parties whose legislation requires the completion of domestic procedures for its entry into force on the date of submission to the depositary of the relevant notification. The Parties shall notify the depositary within three months from the signature of this Treaty of the need to complete such procedures.

Article 23

This Treaty shall remain in force for five years from the date of its entry into force, and shall be automatically extended for further five-year periods unless the Parties adopt another procedure.

Each of the Parties may withdraw from this Treaty by sending written notification thereof to the depositary not less than six months prior to its withdrawal and after settling financial and other obligations that arose during the period for which this Treaty was in force.

The provisions of Article 18 of this Treaty shall continue to be applicable for a Party which withdraws from the Treaty for a further 10 years, and those of Article 10 indefinitely.

Article 24

Following the entry into force of this Treaty, it may with the consent of the Parties be acceded to by other States, including States which are not members of the Commonwealth of Independent States, by means of the transmission to the depositary of instruments of accession. Accession shall be deemed to take effect upon the expiry of 30 days from the date of receipt by the depositary of the latest notification by the Parties of consent to such accession.

Article 25

The depositary shall immediately notify the Parties of an accession to this Treaty or of the completion of domestic procedures required for its entry into force, of the date of entry into force of the Treaty and of the receipt by it of other notifications and documents.

DONE at Minsk on 4 June 1999 in one original in the Russian language. The original shall be kept in the Executive Committee of the Commonwealth of Independent States, which shall send to each State signing this Treaty a true copy thereof.

18. Convention of the Organisation of the Islamic Conference on Combating International Terrorism

Adopted at Ouagadougou on 1 July 1999
Entry into force in accordance with article 40
Depositary: General Secretariat of the Organisation of the Islamic Conference

The Member States of the Organisation of the Islamic Conference,

PURSUANT to the tenets of the tolerant Islamic Sharia which reject all forms of violence and terrorism, and in particular specially those based on extremism and call for protection of human rights, which provisions are paralleled by the principles and rules of international law founded on cooperation between peoples for the establishment of peace;

ABIDING by the lofty, moral and religious principles particularly the provisions of the Islamic Sharia as well as the human heritage of the Islamic Ummah.

ADHERING to the Charter of the Organisation of the Islamic Conference, its objectives and principles aimed at creating an appropriate atmosphere to strengthen cooperation and understanding among Islamic States as well as relevant OIC resolutions;

ADHERING to the principles of International Law and the United Nations Charter as well as all relevant UN resolutions on procedures aimed at eliminating international terrorism, and all other conventions and international instruments to which states acceding to this Convention are parties and which call, inter alia, for the observance of the sovereignty, stability, territorial integrity, political independence and security of states, and non-intervention in their international affairs;

PROCEEDING from the rules of the Code of Conduct of the Organisation of Islamic Conference for Combating International Terrorism;

DESIRING to promote cooperation among them for combating

terrorist crimes that threaten the security and stability of the Islamic States and endanger their vital interests;

BEING COMMITTED to combating all forms and manifestations of terrorism and eliminating its objectives and causes which target the lives and properties of people;

CONFIRMING the legitimacy of the right of peoples to struggle against foreign occupation and colonialist and racist regimes by all means, including armed struggle to liberate their territories and attain their rights to self-determination and independence in compliance with the purposes and principles of the Charter and resolutions of the United Nations;

BELIEVING that terrorism constitutes a gross violation of human rights, in particular the right to freedom and security, as well as an obstacle to the free functioning of institutions and socio-economic development, as it aims at destabilizing States;

CONVINCED that terrorism cannot be justified in any way, and that it should therefore be unambiguously condemned in all its forms and manifestations, and all its actions, means and practices, whatever its origin, causes or purposes, including direct or indirect actions of States;

RECOGNIZING the growing links between terrorism and organized crime, including illicit trafficking in arms, narcotics, human beings and money laundering;

HAVE AGREED to conclude this Convention, calling on all Member States of the Organisation of the Islamic Conference to accede to it.

DEFINITION AND GENERAL PROVISIONS

Article I

For the purposes of this Convention:

1. "Contracting State" or "Contracting Party" means every Member State in the Organisation of the Islamic Conference that has ratified or adhered to this Convention and deposited its instruments of

ratification or adherence with the General Secretariat of the Organisation.

2. "Terrorism" means any act of violence or threat thereof notwithstanding its motives or intentions perpetrated to carry out an individual or collective criminal plan with the aim of terrorizing people or threatening to harm them or imperiling their lives, honour, freedoms, security or rights or exposing the environment or any facility or public or private property to hazards or occupying or seizing them, or endangering a national resource, or international facilities, or threatening the stability, territorial integrity, political unity or sovereignty of independent States.

3. "Terrorist Crime" means any crime executed, started or participated in to realize a terrorist objective in any of the Contracting States or against its nationals, assets or interests or foreign facilities and nationals residing in its territory punishable by its internal law.

4. Crimes stipulated in the following conventions are also considered terrorist crimes with the exception of those excluded by the legislations of Contracting States or those who have not ratified them:

a) Convention on "Offences and Other Acts Committed on Board of Aircrafts" (Tokyo, 14.9.1963).

b) Convention on "Suppression of Unlawful Seizure of Aircraft" (The Hague, 16.12.1970).

c) Convention on "Suppression of Unlawful Acts Against the Safety of Civil Aviation" signed at Montreal on 23.9.1971 and its Protocol (Montreal, 10.12.1984).

d) Convention on the "Prevention and Punishment of Crimes Against Persons Enjoying International Immunity, Including Diplomatic Agents" (New York, 14.12.1973).

e) International Convention Against the Taking of Hostages (New York, 1979).

f) The United Nations Law of the Sea Convention of 1988 and its related provisions on piracy at sea.

g)   Convention on the "Physical Protection of Nuclear Material" (Vienna, 1979).

h)   Protocol for the Suppression of Unlawful Acts of Violence at Airports Serving International Civil Aviation-Supplementary to the Convention for the Suppression of Unlawful Acts Against the Safety of Civil Aviation (Montreal, 1988).

i)   Protocol for the Suppression of Unlawful Acts Against the Safety of Fixed Platforms on the Continental Shelf (Rome, 1988).

j)   Convention for the Suppression of Unlawful Acts Against the Safety of Maritime Navigation (Rome, 1988).

k)   International Convention for the Suppression of Terrorist Bombings (New York, 1997).

l)   Convention on the Marking of Plastic Explosives for the purposes of Detection (Montreal, 1991).

Article 2

a) Peoples' struggle including armed struggle against foreign occupation, aggression, colonialism, and hegemony, aimed at liberation and self-determination in accordance with the principles of international law shall not be considered a terrorist crime.

b) None of the terrorist crimes mentioned in the previous Article shall be considered political crimes.

c) In the implementation of the provisions of this Convention the following crimes shall not be considered political crimes even when politically motivated:

1.   Aggression against kings and heads of state of Contracting States or against their spouses, their ascendants or descendants.

2. Aggression against crown princes or vice-presidents or deputy heads of government or ministers in any of the Contracting States.

3. Aggression against persons enjoying international immunity including Ambassadors and diplomats in Contracting States or in countries of accreditation.

4. Murder or robbery by force against individuals or authorities or means of transport and communications.

5. Acts of sabotage and destruction of public properties and properties geared for public services, even if belonging to another Contracting State.

6. Crimes of manufacturing, smuggling or possessing arms and ammunition or explosives or other materials prepared for committing terrorist crimes.

d) All forms of international crimes, including illegal trafficking in narcotics and human beings and money laundering aimed at financing terrorist objectives shall be considered terrorist crimes.

SECTION II
FOUNDATIONS OF ISLAMIC COOPERATION FOR COMBATING TERRORISM

CHAPTER I
IN THE FIELD OF SECURITY

DIVISION I
MEASURES TO PREVENT AND COMBAT TERRORIST CRIMES

Article 3

I. The Contracting States are committed not to execute, initiate or participate in any form in organizing or financing or committing or instigating or supporting terrorist acts whether directly or indirectly.

191

II. Committed to prevent and combat terrorist crimes in conformity with the provisions of this Convention and their respective domestic rules and regulations the Contracting States shall see to:

(A)   *Preventive Measures:*

1.   Barring their territories from being used as an arena for planning, organizing, executing terrorist crimes or initiating or participating in these crimes in any form; including preventing the infiltration of terrorist elements or their gaining refuge or residence therein individually or collectively, or receiving hosting, training, arming, financing or extending any facilities to them.

2.   Cooperating and coordinating with the rest of the Contracting States, particularly neighbouring countries which suffer from similar or common terrorist crimes.

3.   Developing and strengthening systems relating to detecting transportation, importing, exporting, stockpiling, and using of weapons, ammunition and explosives as well as other means of aggression, killing and destruction in addition to strengthening trans-border and custom controls in order to intercept their transfer from one Contracting State to another or to other States unless they are intended for specific legitimate purposes.

4.   Developing and strengthening systems related to surveillance procedures, securing borders, and land, sea and air passages in order to prevent infiltration through them.

5.   Strengthening systems for ensuring the safety and protection of personalities, vital installations and means of public transport.

6.   Re-enforcing protection, security and safety of diplomatic and consular persons and missions; and regional and international organizations accredited in the Contracting State in accordance with the conventions and rules of international law which govern this subject.

7.   Promoting security intelligence activities and coordinating them with the intelligence activities of each Contracting State pursuant to their respective intelligence policies, aimed at exposing the objectives of terrorist groups and organisations, thwarting their designs and revealing the extent of their danger to security and stability.

8.   Establishing a data base by each Contracting State to collect and analyze data on terrorist elements, groups, movements and organizations and monitor developments of the phenomenon of terrorism and successful experiences in combating it. Moreover, the Contracting State shall update this information and exchange them with competent authorities in other Contracting States within the limits of the laws and regulations in every State.

9.   To take all necessary measures to eliminate and prevent the establishment of webs supporting all kinds of terrorist crimes.

(B)   *Combating Measures:*

1.   Arresting perpetrators of terrorist crimes and prosecuting them according to the national law or extraditing them in accordance with the provisions of this Convention or existing Conventions between the requesting and requested States.

2.   Ensuring effective protection of persons working in the field of criminal justice as well as to witnesses and investigators.

3.   Ensuring effective protection of information sources and witnesses on terrorist crimes.

4.   Extending necessary assistance to victims of terrorism.

5.   Establishing effective cooperation between the concerned organs in the Contracting States and the citizens for combating terrorism including extending appropriate guarantees and appropriate incentives to encourage informing on terrorist acts and submitting information to help uncover them and cooperating in arresting the perpetrators.

DIVISION II

AREAS OF ISLAMIC COOPERATION FOR PREVENTING AND COMBATING TERRORIST CRIMES

Article 4

Contracting States shall cooperate among themselves to prevent and combat terrorist crimes in accordance with the respective laws and regulations of each State in the following areas:

First: Exchange of Information

1. Contracting States shall undertake to promote exchange of information among them as such regarding:

    a)   Activities and crimes committed by terrorist groups, their leaders, their elements, their headquarters, training, means and sources that provide finance and weapons, types of arms, ammunition and explosives utilized as well as other ways and means to attack, kill and destroy.

    b)   Means of communications and propaganda utilized by terrorist groups, how they act, movement of their leaders, their elements and their travel documents.

2. Contracting States shall expeditiously inform any other Contracting State regarding available information about any terrorist crime perpetrated in its territory aimed at undermining the interests of that State or its nationals and to state the facts surrounding the crime in terms of its circumstances, criminals involved, victims, losses, devices and methods utilized to carry out the crime, without prejudicing investigation and inquiry requisites.

3. Contracting States shall exchange information with the other Parties to combat terrorist crimes and to inform the Contracting State or other States of all available information or data that

could prevent terrorist crimes within its territory or against its nationals or residents or interests.

4.   The Contracting States shall provide any other Contracting State with available information or data that will:

   a)   Assist in arresting those accused of committing a terrorist crime against the interests of that country or being implicated in such acts either by assistance, collusion, instigation, or financing.

   b)   Contribute to confiscating any arms, weapons, explosives, devices or funds spent or meant to be spent to commit a terrorist crime.

5.   The Contracting States undertake to respect the confidentiality of information exchanged between them and shall refrain from passing it to any non-Contracting States or other parties without prior consent of the source country.

Second: Investigation

Each Contracting State pledges to promote cooperation with other contracting states and to extend assistance in the field of investigation procedures in terms of arresting escaped suspects or those convicted for terrorist crimes in accordance with the laws and regulations of each country.

Third: Exchange of Expertise

1.   Contracting States shall cooperate with each other to undertake and exchange studies and researches on combating terrorist crimes as well as exchange of expertise in this field.

2.   Contracting States shall cooperate within the scope of their capabilities to provide available technical assistance for preparing programmes or holding joint training sessions with one or more Contracting State if the need arises for personnel required in the field of combating terrorism in order to improve

their scientific and practical potential and upgrade their performance standards.

Fourth: Education and Information Field

The Contracting States shall cooperate in:

1. Promoting information activities and supporting the mass media in order to confront the vicious campaign against Islam, by projecting the true image of tolerance of Islam, and exposing the designs and danger of terrorist groups against the stability and security of Islamic States.

2. Including the noble human values, which proscribe the practice of terrorism in the educational curricula of Contracting States.

3. Supporting efforts aimed at keeping abreast of the age by introducing an advanced Islamic thought based on *ijtihad* by which Islam is distinguished.

CHAPTER II
IN THE JUDICIAL FIELD

SECTION I
EXTRADITING CRIMINALS

Article 5

Contracting States shall undertake to extradite those indicted or convicted of terrorist crimes, requested for extradition by any of these countries in compliance with the rules and conditions stipulated in this Convention.

Article 6

Extradition shall not be permissible in the following cases:
1. If the Crime for which extradition is requested is deemed by the laws enforced in the requested Contracting State as one of a political nature and without prejudice to the provisions of Article

2, paragraphs 2 and 3 of this Convention for which extradition is requested.

2. If the Crime for which extradition is sought relates solely to a dereliction of military obligations.

3. If the Crime for which extradition is requested, was committed in the territory of the requested Contracting State, unless this crime has undermined the interests of the requesting Contracting State and its laws stipulate that the perpetrators of those crimes shall be prosecuted and punished providing that the requested country has not commenced investigation or trial.

4. If the Crime has been the subject of a final sentence which has the force of law in the requested Contracting State.

5. If the action at the time of the extradition request elapsed or the penalty prescribed in accordance with the law in the Contracting State requesting extradition.

6. Crimes committed outside the territory of the requesting Contracting State by a person who was not its national and the law of the requested Contracting State does not prosecute such a crime if perpetrated outside its territory by such a person.

7. If pardon was granted and included the perpetrators of these crimes in the requesting Contracting State.

8. If the legal system of the requested State does not permit extradition of its national, then it shall be obliged to prosecute whosoever commits a terrorist crime if the act is punishable in both States by a freedom-restraining sentence for a minimum period of one year or more. The nationality of the person requested for extradition shall be determined according to the date of the crime taking into account the investigation undertaken in this respect by the requesting State.

Article 7

If the person requested for extradition is under investigation or trial for another crime in the requested State, his extradition shall be postponed until the investigation is disposed of or the trial is over and the punishment implemented. In this case, the requested State shall extradite him provisionally for investigation or trial on condition that he shall be returned to it before execution of the sentence issued in the requested State.

Article 8

For the purpose of extraditing crime perpetrators according to this Convention, the domestic legislations of Contracting States shall not have any bearing as to their differences with respect to the crime being classified as a felony or misdemeanor, nor as to the penalty prescribed for it.

SECTION II
ROGATORY COMMISSION

Article 9

Each Contracting State shall request from any other Contracting State to undertake in its territory rogatory action with respect to any judicial procedures concerning an action involving a terrorist crime and in particular:

1.   To hear witnesses and testimonies taken as evidence.

2.   To communicate legal documents.

3.   To implement inquiry and detention procedures.

4.   To undertake on the scene inspection and analyse evidence.

5.   To obtain necessary evidence or documents or records or their certified copies.

Article 10

Each Contracting State shall implement rogatory commissions related to terrorist crimes and may reject the request for implementation with respect to the following cases.

1. If the crime for which the request is made, is the subject of a charge, investigation or trial in the country requested to implement rogatory commission.

2. If the implementation of the request prejudices the sovereignty or the security or public order of the country charged with this mission.

Article 11

The request for a rogatory commission shall be implemented promptly in accordance with the provisions of the domestic laws of the requested State and which may postpone its implementation until its investigation and prosecution procedures are completed on the same subject or until the compelling reasons that called for postponement are removed. In this case the requesting State shall be informed of this postponement.

Article 12

The request for a rogatory commission related to a terrorist crime shall not be refused on the grounds of the rule of transaction confidentiality for banks and financial institutions. And in the implementation of the request the rules of the enforcing State are to be followed.

Article 13

The procedure, undertaken through a rogatory commission in accordance with the provisions of this Convention, shall have the same legal effect as if it was brought before the competent authority in the State requesting the rogatory commission. The results of its implementation shall only be utilized within the scope of the rogatory commission.

SECTION 3
JUDICIAL COOPERATION

Article 14

Each Contracting State shall extend to the other contracting parties every possible assistance as may be necessary for investigation or trial proceedings related to terrorist crimes.

Article 15

1. If judicial competence accrues to one of the Contracting States for the prosecution of a subject accused of a terrorist crime, this State may request the country which hosts the suspect to prosecute him for this crime subject to the host country's consent and providing the crime is punishable in that country by a freedom restraining sentence for at least one year or by a more severe sanction. In such a case the requesting State shall pass all investigation documents and evidence related to the crime to the requested State.

2. Investigation or trial shall be conducted on the grounds of the case or cases brought by the requesting State against the accused in accordance with the legal provisions and procedures of the country holding the trial.

Article 16

The request for trial on the basis of paragraph (1) of the previous Article, entails the suspension of procedures of prosecution, investigation and trial in the territory of the requesting State except those relating to the requisites of cooperation, assistance or rogatory commission sought by the State requested to hold the trial procedures.

Article 17

1. Procedures undertaken in either of the two States, the requesting State or the one where the trial is held, shall be subject to the law of the country where the procedure is executed and which shall have legal preeminence as may be stipulated in its legislation.

2. The requesting State shall not bring to trial or retrial the accused subject unless the requested State refuses to prosecute him.

3. In all cases the State requested to hold trial shall inform the requesting country of its action with respect to the request for trial and shall communicate to it the results of its investigations or trial proceedings.

Article 18

The State requested to hold trial may undertake all measures and procedures stipulated by its legislation regarding the accused both before and after the request for trial is received.

SECTION 4
SEIZED ASSETS AND PROCEEDS OF THE CRIME

Article 19

1. If the extradition of a subject is decided, the Contracting State shall hand over to the requesting State the assets and proceeds seized, used or related to the terrorist crime, found in the possession of the wanted subject or with a third party.

2. The material mentioned in the previous item shall be handed over even if the accused has not been extradited either due to his escape, death or any other reason after ensuring that these were connected with the terrorist crime.

3. The provisions contained in the two previous items shall not prejudice the rights of any of the Contracting States or bona fide third parties with respect to the above-mentioned assets and proceeds.

Article 20

The State requested to hand over the assets and proceeds may undertake all necessary custodial measures and procedures for the implementation of its obligation. It may also retain them provisionally if required for penal action implemented therein or hand them to the requesting State on condition that they shall be returned for the same purpose.

SECTION 5
EXCHANGE OF EVIDENCE

Article 21

A Contracting State shall see to it that the evidence and effects of any terrorist crime committed on its territory against another Contracting State are examined by its competent organs and may seek assistance to that end from any other Contracting State. Moreover, it shall take every necessary step to safeguard the evidence and proof of their legal relevance. It may communicate, if requested, the result to the country whose interests were targeted by the crime. The State or States which have assisted in this case shall not pass this information to others.

PART III
MECHANISM FOR IMPLEMENTING COOPERATION

CHAPTER I
EXTRADITION PROCEDURES

Article 22

The exchange of extradition requests between Contracting States shall be undertaken directly through diplomatic channels or through their Ministries of Justice or their substitute.

Article 23

A request for extradition shall be submitted in writing and shall include:

1. The original or an authenticated copy of the indictment, arrest order or any other instruments of identical weight issued in line with the conditions stipulated in the requesting State's legislation.

2. A statement of the acts for which extradition is sought specifying
    the dates and places, where these acts were committed and their
    legal implications along with reference to the legal articles under
    which they fall as well as a copy of these articles.

3. Description, in as much detail as possible, of the subject wanted
    for extradition and any other information such as to determine
    his identity and nationality.

Article 24

1. The judicial authorities in the requesting State may approach
the requested State by any channel of written communication and seek the
preventive arrest of the wanted subject pending the arrival of the
extradition request.

2. In this case the requested State may effect the preventive arrest
of the wanted subject. However, if the request for extradition is not
submitted together with the necessary documents listed in the above
Article, the subject whose extradition is sought may not be detained for
more than thirty days as of the day of his arrest.

Article 25

The requesting State shall send a request together with the
documents listed in Article 23 of this Convention. If the requested State
accepts the request as valid, its competent authorities shall implement it
in accordance with its legislation and shall promptly notify the requesting
State of the action undertaken.

Article 26

1. In all cases stipulated in the two Articles above, preventive
detention shall not exceed sixty days after the date of arrest.

2. Temporary release may be effected during the period
stipulated in the previous Article and the requested State shall take
appropriate measures to ensure that the wanted subject does not escape.

3. Release shall not prevent the re-arrest of the subject and his extradition if it was requested after his release.

Article 27

If the requested State requires additional clarification to ascertain the conditions stipulated in this chapter, it shall notify the requesting State thereof and fix a date for provision of such clarifications.

Article 28

If the requested State received a number of extradition requests from various countries related to the same or diverse acts, this State shall decide upon these requests bearing in mind the circumstances and in particular the possibility of subsequent extradition, date of receiving the requests, degree of the danger of the crime and where it was committed.

CHAPTER II
MEASURES FOR ROGATORY COMMISSIONS

Article 29

Rogatory Commission requests must specify the following:

1. The competent authority that issued the request.

2. Subject of the request and its reason.

3. The identity and nationality of the person being the subject of the rogatory commission (as may be possible).

4. Information on the crime requiring the rogatory commission, its legal definition and penalty inflicted on its perpetrators along with maximum available information on its circumstances in order to ensure the efficient implementation of the rogatory commission.

Article 30

1. The request for rogatory commission shall be forwarded by the Ministry of Justice in the requesting State to the Ministry of Justice in the requested State and returned in the same way.

2. In case of expediency, the request for rogatory commission shall be directly forwarded by the judicial authorities in the requesting State to the judicial authorities in the requested State. A copy of this rogatory commission shall also be sent at the same time to the Ministry of Justice in the requested State. The rogatory commission shall be returned together with the papers concerning its implementation in the way stipulated in the previous item.

3. The request for rogatory commission may be forwarded directly from the judicial authorities to the competent authority in the requested country. Answers may be sent directly through the said authority.

Article 31

Requests for rogatory commission and accompanying documents shall be signed or stamped with the seal of a competent authority or that authorized by it. These documents shall be exempted from all formal procedures that could be required by the legislation of the requested State.

Article 32

If the authority that received the request for rogatory commission was not competent enough to deal with it, it shall automatically transfer it to the competent authority in its country. If the request is forwarded directly the answer shall reach the requesting State in the same manner.

Article 33

Any refusal for rogatory commission shall be explained.

CHAPTER III
MEASURES FOR PROTECTING WITNESSES AND EXPERTS

Article 34

If the requesting State deems that the appearance of the witness or expert before its judicial authorities is of special importance, reference thereto shall be made in its request. The request or summons shall include an approximate statement in terms of compensation, travel expenses, accommodation and commitment to make these payments. The requested State shall invite the witness or expert and inform the requesting State about his/her reply.

Article 35

1. No penalty nor coercive measure may be inflicted upon the witness or expert who does not comply with the summons even if the writ provides for such a penalty.

2. If the witness or expert arrives voluntarily to the territory of the requesting State, he shall be summoned according to the provisions of the internal legislation of this State.

Article 36

1. A witness or expert may not be subjected to trial, detained or have his freedom restricted in the territory of the requesting State, for acts or court rulings that preceded his departure for the requesting State, irrespective of his nationality, as long as his appearance before the judicial authorities of the said State is based on a summons.

2. No witness or expert, whatever his nationality, appearing before the judiciary of the State in question on the basis of a summons, may be prosecuted or detained or have his freedom restricted in any way on the requesting State's territory for other acts or court decisions not mentioned in the summons and predating his departure from the State from which he is requested.

3. The immunity privileges stated in this Article shall become invalid if a witness or expert remains on the requesting State's territories for over thirty consecutive days despite his ability to return once his presence was no longer requested by the judiciary, or if he returns to the requesting State's territories after his departure.

Article 37

1. The requesting State shall undertake all necessary measures to ensure the protection of a witness or expert from publicity that could endanger him, his family or his property as a result of his testimony and in particular:

a) To ensure confidentiality of the date and place of his arrival as well as the means involved.

b) To ensure confidentiality of his accommodation, movements and locations where he may be found.

c) To ensure confidentiality of the testimony and information given to the competent judicial authorities.

2. The requesting State shall provide necessary security required by the condition of the witness or expert and of his family, and circumstances of the case and types of expected risks.

Article 38

1. If the witness or expert who is summoned to the requesting State is imprisoned in the requested State, he shall be provisionally transferred to the location of the hearing at which he is to testify according to conditions and times determined by the requested State.

2. Transfer may be denied:

a) If the witness or expert refuses.

b) If his presence is necessary for undertaking criminal procedures in the territory of the requested State.

c) If his transfer would prolong his imprisonment.

d) If there are considerations militating against his transfer.

3. The transferred witness or expert shall remain in detention in the territory of the requesting State until he is repatriated to the requested State unless the latter requests his release.

SECTION IV
FINAL PROVISIONS

Article 39

This Convention shall be ratified, or adhered to, by the Signatory States and the instruments of ratification or accession shall be deposited with the General Secretariat of the Organisation of the Islamic Conference not exceeding a period of thirty days as of the date of ratification or accession. The General Secretariat shall inform all Member States about any deposition and date of such instruments.

Article 40

1. This Convention shall enter into force thirty days after the deposit of the seventh instrument of ratification or accession at the OIC General Secretariat.

2. This Convention shall not be applicable to any other Islamic State until it deposits its instruments of ratification or accession with the General Secretariat of the Organisation of the Islamic Conference and after a period of thirty days of the date of deposition.

Article 41

It is not permissible for any Contracting State to make any reservations, explicitly or implicitly in conflict with the provisions of this Convention or deviating from its objectives.

Article 42

1. A Contracting State shall not withdraw from this Convention except by a written request to the Secretary General of the Organisation of the Islamic Conference.

2. Withdrawal shall be effective six months after the date of sending the request to the Secretary General.

This Convention has been written in English, Arabic and French of equal authenticity, of one original deposited with the General Secretariat of the Organization of the Islamic Conference which shall have it registered at the United Nations Organization, in accordance with the provisions of Article 102 of its Charter. The General Secretariat shall communicate approved copies thereof to the Member States of the Organisation of the Islamic Conference.

19. OAU Convention on the Prevention and Combating of Terrorism, 1999

Adopted at Algiers on 14 July 1999
Entry into force in accordance with Article 20
Depositary: Secretary-General of the Organization of African Unity

The Member States of the Organization of African Unity:

CONSIDERING the purposes and principles enshrined in the Charter of the Organization of African Unity, in particular its clauses relating to the security, stability, development of friendly relations and cooperation among its Member States;

RECALLING the provisions of the Declaration on the Code of Conduct for Inter-African Relations, adopted by the Thirtieth Ordinary Session of the Assembly of Heads of State and Government of the Organization of African Unity, held in Tunis, Tunisia, from 13 to 15 June 1994;

AWARE of the need to promote human and moral values based on tolerance and rejection of all forms of terrorism irrespective of their motivations;

BELIEVINGin the principles of international law, the provisions of the Charters of the Organization of African Unity and of the United Nations and the latter's relevant resolutions on measures aimed at combating international terrorism and, in particular, resolution 49/60 of the General Assembly of 9 December 1994, together with the annexed Declaration on Measures to Eliminate International Terrorism as well as resolution 51/210 of the General Assembly of 17 December 1996 and the Declaration to Supplement the 1994 Declaration on Measures to Eliminate International Terrorism, annexed thereto;

DEEPLY concerned over the scope and seriousness of the phenomenon of terrorism and the dangers it poses to the stability and security of States;

DESIROUS of strengthening cooperation among Member States in order to forestall and combat terrorism;

REAFFIRMING the legitimate right of peoples for self-determination and independence pursuant to the principles of international law and the provisions of the Charters of the Organization of African Unity and the United Nations as well as the African Charter on Human and Peoples' Rights;

CONCERNED that the lives of innocent women and children are most adversely affected by terrorism;

CONVINCED that terrorism constitutes a serious violation of human rights and, in particular, the rights to physical integrity, life, freedom and security, and impedes socio-economic development through destabilization of States;

CONVINCED FURTHER that terrorism cannot be justified under any circumstances and, consequently, should be combated in all its forms and manifestations, including those in which States are involved directly or indirectly, without regard to its origin, causes and objectives;

AWARE of the growing links between terrorism and organized crime, including the illicit traffic of arms, drugs and money laundering;

DETERMINED to eliminate terrorism in all its forms and manifestations;

HAVE AGREED AS FOLLOWS:

PART I
SCOPE OF APPLICATION

Article 1

For the purposes of this Convention:

1. "Convention" means the OAU Convention on the Prevention and Combating of Terrorism.

2. "State Party" means any Member State of the Organization of African Unity which has ratified or acceded to this Convention and has deposited its instrument of ratification or accession with the Secretary General of the Organization of African Unity.

3. "Terrorist act" means:

(*a*)   any act which is a violation of the criminal laws of a State Party and which may endanger the life, physical integrity or freedom of, or cause serious injury or death to, any person, any number or group of persons or causes or may cause damage to public or private property, natural resources, environmental or cultural heritage and is calculated or intended to:

   (i)   intimidate, put in fear, force, coerce or induce any government, body, institution, the general public or any segment thereof, to do or abstain from doing any act, or to adopt or abandon a particular standpoint, or to act according to certain principles; or

   (ii)   disrupt any public service, the delivery of any essential service to the public or to create a public emergency; or

   (iii) create general insurrection in a State;

(*b*)   any promotion, sponsoring, contribution to, command, aid, incitement, encouragement, attempt, threat, conspiracy, organizing, or procurement of any person, with the intent to commit any act referred to in paragraph (a) (i) to (iii).

Article 2

States Parties undertake to:

(*a*)   review their national laws and establish criminal offences for terrorist acts as defined in this Convention and make such acts punishable by appropriate penalties that take into account the grave nature of such offences;

(*b*)   consider, as a matter of priority, the signing or ratification of, or accession to, the international instruments listed in the Annexure, which they have not yet signed, ratified or acceded to; and

(*c*)   implement the actions, including enactment of legislation and the establishment as criminal offences of certain acts as required in terms of the international instruments referred to in paragraph (b) and that States have ratified and acceded to and make such acts punishable by appropriate penalties which take into account the grave nature of those offences;

(*d*)   notify the Secretary General of the OAU of all the legislative measures it has taken and the penalties imposed on terrorist acts within one year of its ratification of, or accession to, the Convention.

Article 3

1. Notwithstanding the provisions of Article 1, the struggle waged by peoples in accordance with the principles of international law for their liberation or self-determination, including armed struggle against colonialism, occupation, aggression and domination by foreign forces shall not be considered as terrorist acts.

2. Political, philosophical, ideological, racial, ethnic, religious or other motives shall not be a justifiable defence against a terrorist act.

PART II
AREAS OF COOPERATION

Article 4

1. States Parties undertake to refrain from any acts aimed at organizing, supporting, financing, committing or inciting to commit terrorist acts, or providing havens for terrorists, directly or indirectly, including the provision of weapons and their stockpiling in their countries and the issuing of visas and travel documents.

2. States Parties shall adopt any legitimate measures aimed at preventing and combating terrorist acts in accordance with the provisions of this Convention and their respective national legislation, in particular, they shall do the following:

(*a*)   prevent their territories from being used as a base for the planning, organization or execution of terrorist acts or for the participation or collaboration in these acts in any form whatsoever;

(*b*)   develop and strengthen methods of monitoring and detecting plans or activities aimed at the illegal cross-border transportation, importation, export, stockpiling and use of arms, ammunition and explosives and other materials and means of committing terrorist acts;

(*c*)   develop and strengthen methods of controlling and monitoring land, sea and air borders and customs and immigration check-points in order to pre-empt any infiltration by individuals or groups involved in the planning, organization and execution of terrorist acts;

(*d*)   strengthen the protection and security of persons, diplomatic and consular missions, premises of regional and international organizations accredited to a State Party, in accordance with the relevant conventions and rules of international law;

(*e*)   promote the exchange of information and expertise on terrorist acts and establish data bases for the collection and analysis of information and data on terrorist elements, groups, movements and organizations;

(*f*)   take all necessary measures to prevent the establishment of terrorist support networks in any form whatsoever;

(*g*)   ascertain, when granting asylum, that the asylum seeker is not involved in any terrorist act;

(*h*)   arrest the perpetrators of terrorist acts and try them in accordance with national legislation, or extradite them in accordance with the provisions of this Convention or extradition treaties concluded between the requesting State and the requested State and, in the absence of a treaty, consider facilitating the extradition of persons suspected of having committed terrorist acts; and

(*i*)   establish effective co-operation between relevant domestic security officials and services and the citizens of the States Parties in a bid to enhance public awareness of the scourge of terrorist acts and the need to combat such acts, by providing guarantees and incentives that will encourage the population to give information on terrorist acts or other acts which may help to uncover such acts and arrest their perpetrators.

Article 5

States Parties shall co-operate among themselves in preventing and combating terrorist acts in conformity with national legislation and procedures of each State in the following areas:

1. States Parties undertake to strengthen the exchange of information among them regarding:

(*a*)   acts and crimes committed by terrorist groups, their leaders and elements, their headquarters and training camps, their means and sources of funding and acquisition of arms, the types of arms, ammunition and explosives used, and other means in their possession;

(*b*)   the communication and propaganda methods and techniques used by the terrorists groups, the behaviour of these groups, the movement of their leaders and elements, as well as their travel documents.

2. States Parties undertake to exchange any information that leads to:

215

(*a*)   the arrest of any person charged with a terrorist act against the interests of a State Party or against its nationals, or attempted to commit such an act or participated in it as an accomplice or an instigator;

(*b*)   the seizure and confiscation of any type of arms, ammunition, explosives, devices or funds or other instrumentalities of crime used to commit a terrorist act or intended for that purpose.

3. States Parties undertake to respect the confidentiality of the information exchanged among them and not to provide such information to another State that is not party to this Convention, or to a third State Party, without the prior consent of the State from where such information originated.

4. States Parties undertake to promote co-operation among themselves and to help each other with regard to procedures relating to the investigation and arrest of persons suspected of, charged with or convicted of terrorist acts, in conformity with the national law of each State.

5. States Parties shall co-operate among themselves in conducting and exchanging studies and researches on how to combat terrorist acts and to exchange expertise relating to control of terrorist acts.

6. States Parties shall co-operate among themselves, where possible, in providing any available technical assistance in drawing up programmes or organizing, where necessary and for the benefit of their personnel, joint training courses involving one or several States Parties in the area of control of terrorist acts, in order to improve their scientific, technical and operational capacities to prevent and combat such acts.

PART III
STATE JURISDICTION

Article 6

1. Each State Party has jurisdiction over terrorist acts as defined in Article 1 when:

(a)   the act is committed in the territory of that State and the perpetrator of the act is arrested in its territory or outside it if this is punishable by its national law;

(b)   the act is committed on board a vessel or a ship flying the flag of that State or an aircraft which is registered under the laws of that State at the time the offence is committed; or

(c)   the act is committed by a national or a group of nationals of that State.

2. A State Party may also establish its jurisdiction over any such offence when:

(a)   the act is committed against a national of that State; or

(b)   the act is committed against a State or government facility of that State abroad, including an embassy or other diplomatic or consular premises, and any other property, of that State; or

(c)   the act is committed by a stateless person who has his or her habitual residence in the territory of that State; or

(d)   the act is committed on board an aircraft which is operated by any carrier of that State; and

(e)   the act is committed against the security of the State Party.

3. Upon ratifying or acceding to this Convention, each State Party shall notify the Secretary General of the Organization of African Unity of the jurisdiction it has established in accordance with paragraph 2 under its national law. Should any change take place, the State Party concerned shall immediately notify the Secretary General.

4. Each State Party shall likewise take such measures as may be necessary to establish its jurisdiction over the acts set forth in Article 1 in cases where the alleged offender is present in its territory and it does not extradite that person to any of the States Parties which have established their jurisdiction in accordance with paragraphs 1 or 2.

Article 7

1. Upon receiving information that a person who has committed or who is alleged to have committed any terrorist act as defined in Article 1 may be present in its territory, the State Party concerned shall take such measures as may be necessary under its national law to investigate the facts contained in the information.

2. Upon being satisfied that the circumstances so warrant, the State Party in whose territory the offender or alleged offender is present shall take the appropriate measures under its national law so as to ensure that person's presence for the purpose of prosecution.

3. Any person against whom the measures referred to in paragraph 2 are being taken shall be entitled to:

(*a*)   communicate without delay with the nearest appropriate representative of the State of which that person is a national or which is otherwise entitled to protect that person's rights or, if that person is a stateless person, the State in whose territory that person habitually resides;

(*b*)   be visited by a representative of that State;

(*c*)   be assisted by a lawyer of his or her choice;

(*d*)   be informed of his or her rights under sub-paragraphs (*a*), (*b*) and (*c*).

4. The rights referred to in paragraph 3 shall be exercised in conformity with the national law of the State in whose territory the offender or alleged offender is present, subject to the provision that the said laws must enable full effect to be given to the purposes for which the rights accorded under paragraph 3 are intended.

PART IV
EXTRADITION

Article 8

1. Subject to the provisions of paragraphs 2 and 3 of this Article, the States Parties shall undertake to extradite any person charged with or convicted of any terrorist act carried out on the territory of another State Party and whose extradition is requested by one of the States Parties in conformity with the rules and conditions provided for in this Convention or under extradition agreements between the States Parties and within the limits of their national laws.

2. Any State Party may, at the time of the deposit of its instrument of ratification or accession, transmit to the Secretary General of the OAU the grounds on which extradition may not be granted and shall at the same time indicate the legal basis in its national legislation or international conventions to which it is a party which excludes such extradition. The Secretary General shall forward these grounds to the States Parties.

3. Extradition shall not be granted if final judgement has been passed by a competent authority of the requested State upon the person in respect of the terrorist act or acts for which extradition is requested. Extradition may also be refused if the competent authority of the requested State has decided either not to institute or terminate proceedings in respect of the same act or acts.

4. A State Party in whose territory an alleged offender is present shall be obliged, whether or not the offence was committed in its territory, to submit the case without undue delay to its competent authorities for the purpose of prosecution if it does not extradite that person.

Article 9

Each State Party undertakes to include as an extraditable offence any terrorist act as defined in Article 1, in any extradition treaty existing between any of the States Parties before or after the entry into force of this Convention.

Article 10

Exchange of extradition requests between the States Parties to this Convention shall be effected directly either through diplomatic channels or other appropriate organs in the concerned States.

Article 11

Extradition requests shall be in writing, and shall be accompanied in particular by the following:

(*a*)   an original or authenticated copy of the sentence, warrant of arrest or any order or other judicial decision made, in accordance with the procedures laid down in the laws of the requesting State;

(*b*)   a statement describing the offences for which extradition is being requested, indicating the date and place of its commission, the offence committed, any convictions made and a copy of the provisions of the applicable law; and

(*c*)   as comprehensive a description as possible of the wanted person together with any other information which may assist in establishing the person's identity and nationality.

Article 12

In urgent cases, the competent authority of the State making the extradition may, in writing, request that the State seized of the extradition request arrest the person in question provisionally. Such provisional arrest shall be for a reasonable period in accordance with the national law of the requested State.

Article 13

1. Where a State Party receives several extradition requests from different States Parties in respect of the same suspect and for the same or different terrorist acts, it shall decide on these requests having regard to all the prevailing circumstances, particularly the possibility of subsequent

extradition, the respective dates of receipt of the requests, and the degree of seriousness of the crime.

2. Upon agreeing to extradite, States Parties shall seize and transmit all funds and related materials purportedly used in the commission of the terrorist act to the requesting State as well as relevant incriminating evidence.

3. Such funds, incriminating evidence and related materials, upon confirmation of their use in the terrorist act by the requested State, shall be transmitted to the requesting State even if, for reasons of death or escape of the accused, the extradition in question cannot take place.

4. The provisions in paragraphs 1, 2 and 3 of this Article shall not affect the rights of any of the States Parties or bona fide third parties regarding the materials or revenues mentioned above.

PART V
EXTRA-TERRITORIAL INVESTIGATIONS (COMMISSION
ROGATOIRE) AND MUTUAL LEGAL ASSISTANCE

Article 14

1. Any State Party may, while recognizing the sovereign rights of States Parties in matters of criminal investigation, request any other State Party to carry out, with its assistance and cooperation, on the latter's territory, criminal investigations related to any judicial proceedings concerning alleged terrorist acts and, in particular:

(*a*)   the examination of witnesses and transcripts of statements made as evidence;

(*b*)   the opening of judicial information;

(*c*)   the initiation of investigation processes;

(*d*)   the collection of documents and recordings or, in their absence, authenticated copies thereof;

221

(*e*)   conducting inspections and tracing of assets for evidentiary purposes;

(*f*)   executing searches and seizures; and

(*g*)   service of judicial documents.

Article 15

A commission rogatoire may be refused:

(*a*)   where each of the States Parties has to execute a commission rogatoire relating to the same terrorist acts;

(*b*)   if that request may affect efforts to expose crimes, impede investigations or the indictment of the accused in the country requesting the commission rogatoire; or

(*c*)   if the execution of the request would affect the sovereignty of the requested State, its security or public order.

Article 16

The extra-territorial investigation (commission rogatoire) shall be executed in compliance with the provisions of national laws of the requested State.   The request for an extra-territorial investigation (commission rogatoire) relating to a terrorist act shall not be rejected on the grounds of the principle of confidentiality of bank operations or financial institutions, where applicable.

Article 17

The States Parties shall extend to each other the best possible mutual police and judicial assistance for any investigation, criminal prosecution or extradition proceedings relating to the terrorist acts as set forth in this Convention.

Article 18

The States Parties undertake to develop, if necessary, especially by concluding bilateral and multilateral agreements and arrangements, mutual legal assistance procedures aimed at facilitating and speeding up investigations and collecting evidence, as well as cooperation between law enforcement agencies in order to detect and prevent terrorist acts.

PART VI
FINAL PROVISIONS

Article 19

1. This Convention shall be open to signature, ratification or accession by the Member States of the Organization of African Unity.

2. The instruments of ratification or accession to the present Convention shall be deposited with the Secretary General of the Organization of African Unity.

3. The Secretary General of the Organization of African Unity shall inform Member States of the Organization of the deposit of each instrument of ratification or accession.

4. No State Party may enter a reservation which is incompatible with the object and purposes of this Convention.

5. No State Party may withdraw from this Convention except on the basis of a written request addressed to the Secretary General of the Organization of African Unity. The withdrawal shall take effect six months after the date of receipt of the written request by the Secretary General of the Organization of African Unity.

Article 20

1. This Convention shall enter into force thirty days after the deposit of the fifteenth instrument of ratification with the Secretary General of the Organization of African Unity.

2. For each of the States that shall ratify or accede to this Convention shall enter into force thirty days after the date of the deposit by that State Party of its instrument of ratification or accession.

Article 21

1. Special protocols or agreements may, if necessary, supplement the provisions of this Convention.

2. This Convention may be amended if a State Party makes a written request to that effect to the Secretary General of the Organization of African Unity. The Assembly of Heads of State and Government may only consider the proposed amendment after all the States Parties have been duly informed of it at least three months in advance.

3. The amendment shall be approved by a simple majority of the States Parties. It shall come into force for each State which has accepted it in accordance with its constitutional procedures three months after the Secretary General has received notice of the acceptance.

Article 22

1. Nothing in this Convention shall be interpreted as derogating from the general principles of international law, in particular the principles of international humanitarian law, as well as the African Charter on Human and Peoples' Rights.

2. Any dispute that may arise between the States Parties regarding the interpretation or application of this Convention shall be amicably settled by direct agreement between them. Failing such settlement, any one of the States Parties may refer the dispute to the International Court of Justice in conformity with the Statute of the Court or by arbitration by other States Parties to this Convention.

Article 23

The original of this Convention, of which the Arabic, English, French and Portuguese texts are equally authentic, shall be deposited with the Secretary General of the Organization of African Unity.

ANNEX
LIST OF INTERNATIONAL INSTRUMENTS

(a)   Tokyo Convention on Offences and Certain Other Acts Committed on Board Aircraft of 1963;

(b)   Montreal Convention for the Suppression of Unlawful Acts against the Safety of Civil Aviation of 1971 and the Protocol thereto of 1984;

(c)   New York Convention on the Prevention and Punishment of Crimes against Internationally Protected Persons, including Diplomatic Agents of 1973;

(d)   International Convention against the Taking of Hostages of 1979;

(e)   Convention on the Physical Protection of Nuclear Material of 1979;

(f)   United Nations Convention on the Law of the Sea 1982;

(g)   Protocol for the Suppression of Unlawful Acts of Violence at Airports Serving International Civil Aviation, supplementary to the Convention for the Suppression of Unlawful Acts against the Safety of Civil Aviation of 1988;

(h)   Protocol for the Suppression of Unlawful Acts against the Safety of Fixed Platforms located on the Continental Shelf of 1988;

(i)   Convention for the Suppression of Unlawful Acts against Maritime Navigation of 1988;

(j)   Convention on the Marking of Plastic Explosives of 1991;

(k)   International Convention for the Suppression of Terrorist Explosive Bombs of 1997;

(l)   Convention on the Prohibition of the Use, Stockpiling,

Production and Transfer of Anti-Personnel Mines and on their Destruction of 1997.

PART III

UNITED NATIONS DECLARATIONS

20. Declaration on Measures to Eliminate International Terrorism

General Assembly resolution 49/60 of 9 December 1994, Annex

THE GENERAL ASSEMBLY,

GUIDED by the purposes and principles of the Charter of the United Nations,

RECALLING the Declaration on Principles of International Law concerning Friendly Relations and Cooperation among States in accordance with the Charter of the United Nations,[3] the Declaration on the Strengthening of International Security,[4] the Definition of Aggression,[5] the Declaration on the Enhancement of the Effectiveness of the Principle of Refraining from the Threat or Use of Force in International Relations,[6] the Vienna Declaration and Programme of Action, adopted by the World Conference on Human Rights,[7] the International Covenant on Economic, Social and Cultural Rights[8] and the International Covenant on Civil and Political Rights,[6]

DEEPLY DISTURBED by the world-wide persistence of acts of international terrorism in all its forms and manifestations, including those in which States are directly or indirectly involved, which endanger or take innocent lives, have a deleterious effect on international relations and may

---

[3] Resolution 2625 (XXV), annex .

[4] Resolution 2734 (XXV).

[5] Resolution 3314 (XXIX), annex.

[6] Resolution 42/22, annex.

[7] Report of the World Conference on Human Rights, Vienna, 14-25 June 1993 (A/CONF.157/24 (Part I)), chap. III.

[8] See resolution 2200 A (XXI), annex.

jeopardize the security of States,

DEEPLY CONCERNED by the increase, in many regions of the world, of acts of terrorism based on intolerance or extremism,

CONCERNED at the growing and dangerous links between terrorist groups and drug traffickers and their paramilitary gangs, which have resorted to all types of violence, thus endangering the constitutional order of States and violating basic human rights,

CONVINCED of the desirability for closer coordination and cooperation among States in combating crimes closely connected with terrorism, including drug trafficking, unlawful arms trade, money laundering and smuggling of nuclear and other potentially deadly materials, and bearing in mind the role that could be played by both the United Nations and regional organizations in this respect,

FIRMLY DETERMINED to eliminate international terrorism in all its forms and manifestations,

CONVINCED ALSO that the suppression of acts of international terrorism, including those in which States are directly or indirectly involved, is an essential element for the maintenance of international peace and security,

CONVINCED FURTHER that those responsible for acts of international terrorism must be brought to justice,

STRESSING the imperative need to further strengthen international cooperation between States in order to take and adopt practical and effective measures to prevent, combat and eliminate all forms of terrorism that affect the international community as a whole,

CONSCIOUS of the important role that might be played by the United Nations, the relevant specialized agencies and States in fostering widespread cooperation in preventing and combating international terrorism, *inter alia*, by increasing public awareness of the problem,

RECALLING the existing international treaties relating to various aspects of the problem of international terrorism, *inter alia*, the

Convention on Offences and Certain Other Acts Committed on Board Aircraft, signed at Tokyo on 14 September 1963,[9] the Convention for the Suppression of Unlawful Seizure of Aircraft, signed at The Hague on 16 December 1970,[10] the Convention for the Suppression of Unlawful Acts against the Safety of Civil Aviation, concluded at Montreal on 23 September 1971,[11] the Convention on the Prevention and Punishment of Crimes against Internationally Protected Persons, including Diplomatic Agents, adopted in New York on 14 December 1973,[12] the International Convention against the Taking of Hostages, adopted in New York on 17 December 1979,[13] the Convention on the Physical Protection of Nuclear Material, adopted at Vienna on 3 March 1980,[14] the Protocol for the Suppression of Unlawful Acts of Violence at Airports Serving International Civil Aviation, supplementary to the Convention for the Suppression of Unlawful Acts against the Safety of Civil Aviation, signed at Montreal on 24 February 1988,[15] the Convention for the Suppression of Unlawful Acts against the Safety of Maritime Navigation, done at Rome on 10 March 1988,[16] the Protocol for the Suppression of Unlawful Acts against the Safety of Fixed Platforms located on the Continental Shelf, done at Rome on 10 March 1988,[17] and the Convention on the Marking of Plastic Explosives for the Purpose of Detection, done at Montreal on

[9] United Nations, Treaty Series, vol. 704, No. 10106.

[10] Ibid., vol. 860, No. 12325.

[11] Ibid., vol. 974, No. 14118.

[12] Ibid., vol. 1035, No. 15410.

[13] Resolution 34/146, annex.

[14] International Atomic Energy Agency, document INFCIRC/225; to be published in United Nations, Treaty Series, vol. 1456, No. 24631.

[15] International Civil Aviation Organization, document DOC 9518.

[16] International Maritime Organization, document SUA/CONF/15/Rev.1.

[17] Ibid., document SUA/CONF/16/Rev.2.

1 March 1991,[18]

WELCOMING the conclusion of regional agreements and mutually agreed declarations to combat and eliminate terrorism in all its forms and manifestations,

CONVINCED of the desirability of keeping under review the scope of existing international legal provisions to combat terrorism in all its forms and manifestations, with the aim of ensuring a comprehensive legal framework for the prevention and elimination of terrorism,

SOLEMNLY DECLARES the following:

I

1. The States Members of the United Nations solemnly reaffirm their unequivocal condemnation of all acts, methods and practices of terrorism, as criminal and unjustifiable, wherever and by whomever committed, including those which jeopardize the friendly relations among States and peoples and threaten the territorial integrity and security of States;

2. Acts, methods and practices of terrorism constitute a grave violation of the purposes and principles of the United Nations, which may pose a threat to international peace and security, jeopardize friendly relations among States, hinder international cooperation and aim at the destruction of human rights, fundamental freedoms and the democratic bases of society;

3. Criminal acts intended or calculated to provoke a state of terror in the general public, a group of persons or particular persons for political purposes are in any circumstance unjustifiable, whatever the considerations of a political, philosophical, ideological, racial, ethnic, religious or any other nature that may be invoked to justify them;

---

[18] See S/22393 and Corr.1.

II

4. States, guided by the purposes and principles of the Charter of the United Nations and other relevant rules of international law, must refrain from organizing, instigating, assisting or participating in terrorist acts in territories of other States, or from acquiescing in or encouraging activities within their territories directed towards the commission of such acts;

5. States must also fulfil their obligations under the Charter of the United Nations and other provisions of international law with respect to combating international terrorism and are urged to take effective and resolute measures in accordance with the relevant provisions of international law and international standards of human rights for the speedy and final elimination of international terrorism, in particular:

(*a*)   To refrain from organizing, instigating, facilitating, financing, encouraging or tolerating terrorist activities and to take appropriate practical measures to ensure that their respective territories are not used for terrorist installations or training camps, or for the preparation or organization of terrorist acts intended to be committed against other States or their citizens;

(*b*)   To ensure the apprehension and prosecution or extradition of perpetrators of terrorist acts, in accordance with the relevant provisions of their national law;

(*c*)   To endeavour to conclude special agreements to that effect on a bilateral, regional and multilateral basis, and to prepare, to that effect, model agreements on cooperation;

(*d*)   To cooperate with one another in exchanging relevant information concerning the prevention and combating of terrorism;

(*e*)   To take promptly all steps necessary to implement the existing international conventions on this subject to which they are parties, including the harmonization of their domestic legislation with those conventions;

(*f*)   To take appropriate measures, before granting asylum, for the purpose of ensuring that the asylum seeker has not engaged in terrorist activities and, after granting asylum, for the purpose of ensuring that the refugee status is not used in a manner contrary to the provisions set out in subparagraph (a) above;

6. In order to combat effectively the increase in, and the growing international character and effects of, acts of terrorism, States should enhance their cooperation in this area through, in particular, systematizing the exchange of information concerning the prevention and combating of terrorism, as well as by effective implementation of the relevant international conventions and conclusion of mutual judicial assistance and extradition agreements on a bilateral, regional and multilateral basis;

7. In this context, States are encouraged to review urgently the scope of the existing international legal provisions on the prevention, repression and elimination of terrorism in all its forms and manifestations, with the aim of ensuring that there is a comprehensive legal framework covering all aspects of the matter;

8. Furthermore States that have not yet done so are urged to consider, as a matter of priority, becoming parties to the international conventions and protocols relating to various aspects of international terrorism referred to in the preamble to the present Declaration;

III

9. The United Nations, the relevant specialized agencies and intergovernmental organizations and other relevant bodies must make every effort with a view to promoting measures to combat and eliminate acts of terrorism and to strengthening their role in this field;

10. The Secretary-General should assist in the implementation of the present Declaration by taking, within existing resources, the following practical measures to enhance international cooperation:

(*a*)   A collection of data on the status and implementation of existing multilateral, regional and bilateral agreements relating to international terrorism, including information on incidents caused by international terrorism and criminal prosecutions and sentencing, based on information received from the depositaries of those agreements and from Member States;

(b)   A compendium of national laws and regulations regarding the prevention and suppression of international terrorism in all its forms and manifestations, based on information received from Member States;

(c)   An analytical review of existing international legal instruments relating to international terrorism, in order to assist States in identifying aspects of this matter that have not been covered by such instruments and could be addressed to develop further a comprehensive legal framework of conventions dealing with international terrorism;

(d)   A review of existing possibilities within the United Nations system for assisting States in organizing workshops and training courses on combating crimes connected with international terrorism;

IV

11. All States are urged to promote and implement in good faith and effectively the provisions of the present Declaration in all its aspects;

12. Emphasis is placed on the need to pursue efforts aiming at eliminating definitively all acts of terrorism by the strengthening of international cooperation and progressive development of international law and its codification, as well as by enhancement of coordination between, and increase of the efficiency of, the United Nations and the relevant specialized agencies, organizations and bodies.

21. Declaration to Supplement the 1994 Declaration on Measures to Eliminate International Terrorism

General Assembly resolution 51/210 of 17 December 1996, Annex

THE GENERAL ASSEMBLY,

GUIDED by the purposes and principles of the Charter of the United Nations,

RECALLING the Declaration on Measures to Eliminate International Terrorism adopted by the General Assembly by its resolution 49/60 of 9 December 1994,

RECALLING ALSO the Declaration on the Occasion of the Fiftieth Anniversary of the United Nations,[19]

DEEPLY DISTURBED by the worldwide persistence of acts of international terrorism in all its forms and manifestations, including those in which States are directly or indirectly involved, which endanger or take innocent lives, have a deleterious effect on international relations and may jeopardize the security of States,

UNDERLINING the importance of States developing extradition agreements or arrangements as necessary in order to ensure that those responsible for terrorist acts are brought to justice,

NOTING that the Convention relating to the Status of Refugees,[20] done at Geneva on 28 July 1951, does not provide a basis for the protection of perpetrators of terrorist acts, noting also in this context Articles 1, 2, 32 and 33 of the Convention, and emphasizing in this regard the need for States parties to ensure the proper application of the Convention,

---

[19] See resolution 50/6.

[20] United Nations, Treaty Series, vol. 189, No. 2545.

STRESSING the importance of full compliance by States with their obligations under the provisions of the 1951 Convention[18] and the 1967 Protocol relating to the Status of Refugees,[21] including the principle of non-refoulement of refugees to places where their life or freedom would be threatened on account of their race, religion, nationality, membership in a particular social group or political opinion, and affirming that the present Declaration does not affect the protection afforded under the terms of the Convention and Protocol and other provisions of international law,

RECALLING Article 4 of the Declaration on Territorial Asylum adopted by the General Assembly by its resolution 2312 (XXII) of 14 December 1967,

STRESSING the need further to strengthen international cooperation between States in order to prevent, combat and eliminate terrorism in all its forms and manifestations,

SOLEMNLY DECLARES the following:

1. The States Members of the United Nations solemnly reaffirm their unequivocal condemnation of all acts, methods and practices of terrorism as criminal and unjustifiable, wherever and by whomsoever committed, including those which jeopardize friendly relations among States and peoples and threaten the territorial integrity and security of States;

2. The States Members of the United Nations reaffirm that acts, methods and practices of terrorism are contrary to the purposes and principles of the United Nations; they declare that knowingly financing, planning and inciting terrorist acts are also contrary to the purposes and principles of the United Nations;

3. The States Members of the United Nations reaffirm that States should take appropriate measures in conformity with the relevant provisions of national and international law, including international standards of human rights, before granting refugee status, for the purpose of ensuring that the asylum-seeker has not participated in terrorist acts,

---

[21] Ibid., vol. 606, No. 8791.

considering in this regard relevant information as to whether the asylum-seeker is subject to investigation for or is charged with or has been convicted of offences connected with terrorism and, after granting refugee status, for the purpose of ensuring that that status is not used for the purpose of preparing or organizing terrorist acts intended to be committed against other States or their citizens;

4. The States Members of the United Nations emphasize that asylum-seekers who are awaiting the processing of their asylum applications may not thereby avoid prosecution for terrorist acts;

5. The States Members of the United Nations reaffirm the importance of ensuring effective cooperation between Member States so that those who have participated in terrorist acts, including their financing, planning or incitement, are brought to justice; they stress their commitment, in conformity with the relevant provisions of international law, including international standards of human rights, to work together to prevent, combat and eliminate terrorism and to take all appropriate steps under their domestic laws either to extradite terrorists or to submit the cases to their competent authorities for the purpose of prosecution;

6. In this context, and while recognizing the sovereign rights of States in extradition matters, States are encouraged, when concluding or applying extradition agreements, not to regard as political offences excluded from the scope of those agreements offences connected with terrorism which endanger or represent a physical threat to the safety and security of persons, whatever the motives which may be invoked to justify them;

7. States are also encouraged, even in the absence of a treaty, to consider facilitating the extradition of persons suspected of having committed terrorist acts, insofar as their national laws permit;

8. The States Members of the United Nations emphasize the importance of taking steps to share expertise and information about terrorists, their movements, their support and their weapons and to share information regarding the investigation and prosecution of terrorist acts.

PART IV

OTHER INSTRUMENTS

22. Convention on the Safety of United Nations and Associated Personnel

Adopted by the General Assembly on 9 December 1994
In force on 15 January 1999
U.N. Doc. A/RES/49/59, Annex
Depositary: Secretary-General of the United Nations

THE STATES PARTIES TO THIS CONVENTION,

DEEPLY CONCERNED over the growing number of deaths and injuries resulting from deliberate attacks against United Nations and associated personnel,

BEARING IN MIND that attacks against, or other mistreatment of, personnel who act on behalf of the United Nations are unjustifiable and unacceptable, by whomsoever committed,

RECOGNIZING that United Nations operations are conducted in the common interest of the international community and in accordance with the principles and purposes of the Charter of the United Nations,

ACKNOWLEDGING the important contribution that United Nations and associated personnel make in respect of United Nations efforts in the fields of preventive diplomacy, peacemaking, peace-keeping, peace-building and humanitarian and other operations,

CONSCIOUS of the existing arrangements for ensuring the safety of United Nations and associated personnel, including the steps taken by the principal organs of the United Nations, in this regard,

RECOGNIZING none the less that existing measures of protection for United Nations and associated personnel are inadequate,

ACKNOWLEDGING that the effectiveness and safety of United Nations operations are enhanced where such operations are conducted with the consent and cooperation of the host State,

APPEALING to all States in which United Nations and associated personnel are deployed and to all others on whom such personnel may rely, to provide comprehensive support aimed at facilitating the conduct and fulfilling the mandate of United Nations operations,

CONVINCED that there is an urgent need to adopt appropriate and effective measures for the prevention of attacks committed against United Nations and associated personnel and for the punishment of those who have committed such attacks,

HAVE AGREED AS FOLLOWS:

Article 1
Definitions

For the purposes of this Convention:

(a)   "United Nations personnel" means:

(i)   Persons engaged or deployed by the Secretary-General of the United Nations as members of the military, police or civilian components of a United Nations operation;

(ii)   Other officials and experts on mission of the United Nations or its specialized agencies or the International Atomic Energy Agency who are present in an official capacity in the area where a United Nations operation is being conducted;

(b)   "Associated personnel" means:

(i)   Persons assigned by a Government or an intergovernmental organization with the agreement of the competent organ of the United Nations;

(ii)   Persons engaged by the Secretary-General of the United Nations or by a specialized agency or by the International Atomic Energy Agency;

(iii)   Persons deployed by a humanitarian non-governmental organization or agency under an agreement with the Secretary-General of the United Nations or with a specialized agency or with the International Atomic Energy Agency,

to carry out activities in support of the fulfilment of the mandate of a United Nations operation;

(c)   "United Nations operation" means an operation established by the competent organ of the United Nations in accordance with the Charter of the United Nations and conducted under United Nations authority and control:

    (i)   Where the operation is for the purpose of maintaining or restoring international peace and security; or

    (ii)   Where the Security Council or the General Assembly has declared, for the purposes of this Convention, that there exists an exceptional risk to the safety of the personnel participating in the operation;

(d)   "Host State" means a State in whose territory a United Nations operation is conducted;

(e)   "Transit State" means a State, other than the host State, in whose territory United Nations and associated personnel or their equipment are in transit or temporarily present in connection with a United Nations operation.

Article 2
Scope of application

1. This Convention applies in respect of United Nations and associated personnel and United Nations operations, as defined in Article 1.

2. This Convention shall not apply to a United Nations operation authorized by the Security Council as an enforcement action under Chapter VII of the Charter of the United Nations in which any of the personnel are engaged as combatants against organized armed forces and to which the law of international armed conflict applies.

Article 3
Identification

1. The military and police components of a United Nations operation and their vehicles, vessels and aircraft shall bear distinctive identification. Other personnel, vehicles, vessels and aircraft involved in the United Nations operation shall be appropriately identified unless otherwise decided by the Secretary-General of the United Nations.

2. All United Nations and associated personnel shall carry appropriate identification documents.

Article 4
Agreements on the status of the operation

The host State and the United Nations shall conclude as soon as possible an agreement on the status of the United Nations operation and all personnel engaged in the operation including, *inter alia*, provisions on privileges and immunities for military and police components of the operation.

Article 5
Transit

A transit State shall facilitate the unimpeded transit of United Nations and associated personnel and their equipment to and from the host State.

Article 6
Respect for laws and regulations

1. Without prejudice to such privileges and immunities as they may enjoy or to the requirements of their duties, United Nations and associated personnel shall:

(a) Respect the laws and regulations of the host State and the transit State; and

(b) Refrain from any action or activity incompatible with the impartial and international nature of their duties.

2. The Secretary-General of the United Nations shall take all appropriate measures to ensure the observance of these obligations.

Article 7
Duty to ensure the safety and security of United Nations and associated personnel

1. United Nations and associated personnel, their equipment and premises shall not be made the object of attack or of any action that prevents them from discharging their mandate.

2. States Parties shall take all appropriate measures to ensure the safety and security of United Nations and associated personnel. In particular, States Parties shall take all appropriate steps to protect United Nations and associated personnel who are deployed in their territory from the crimes set out in Article 9.

3. States Parties shall cooperate with the United Nations and other States Parties, as appropriate, in the implementation of this Convention, particularly in any case where the host State is unable itself to take the required measures.

Article 8
Duty to release or return United Nations and associated personnel captured or detained

Except as otherwise provided in an applicable status-of-forces agreement, if United Nations or associated personnel are captured or detained in the course of the performance of their duties and their identification has been established, they shall not be subjected to interrogation and they shall be promptly released and returned to United Nations or other appropriate authorities. Pending their release such personnel shall be treated in accordance with universally recognized standards of human rights and the principles and spirit of the Geneva Conventions of 1949.

Article 9
Crimes against United Nations and associated personnel

1. The intentional commission of:

(*a*)   A murder, kidnapping or other attack upon the person or liberty of any United Nations or associated personnel;

(*b*)   A violent attack upon the official premises, the private accommodation or the means of transportation of any United Nations or associated personnel likely to endanger his or her person or liberty;

(*c*)   A threat to commit any such attack with the objective of compelling a physical or juridical person to do or to refrain from doing any act;

(*d*)   An attempt to commit any such attack; and

(*e*)   An act constituting participation as an accomplice in any such attack, or in an attempt to commit such attack, or in organizing or ordering others to commit such attack,

shall be made by each State Party a crime under its national law.

2. Each State Party shall make the crimes set out in paragraph 1 punishable by appropriate penalties which shall take into account their grave nature.

Article 10
Establishment of jurisdiction

1. Each State Party shall take such measures as may be necessary to establish its jurisdiction over the crimes set out in Article 9 in the following cases:

(*a*)   When the crime is committed in the territory of that State or on board a ship or aircraft registered in that State;

(*b*)   When the alleged offender is a national of that State.

2. A State Party may also establish its jurisdiction over any such crime when it is committed:

(*a*)   By a stateless person whose habitual residence is in that State; or

247

(*b*)   With respect to a national of that State; or

(*c*)   In an attempt to compel that State to do or to abstain from doing
         any act.

3. Any State Party which has established jurisdiction as mentioned in paragraph 2 shall notify the Secretary-General of the United Nations. If such State Party subsequently rescinds that jurisdiction, it shall notify the Secretary-General of the United Nations.

4. Each State Party shall take such measures as may be necessary to establish its jurisdiction over the crimes set out in Article 9 in cases where the alleged offender is present in its territory and it does not extradite such person pursuant to Article 15 to any of the States Parties which have established their jurisdiction in accordance with paragraph 1 or 2.

5. This Convention does not exclude any criminal jurisdiction exercised in accordance with national law.

Article 11
Prevention of crimes against United Nations and associated personnel

States Parties shall cooperate in the prevention of the crimes set out in Article 9, particularly by:

(*a*)   Taking all practicable measures to prevent preparations in their
         respective territories for the commission of those crimes within
         or outside their territories; and

(*b*)   Exchanging information in accordance with their national law
         and coordinating the taking of administrative and other measures
         as appropriate to prevent the commission of those crimes.

Article 12
Communication of information

1. Under the conditions provided for in its national law, the State Party in whose territory a crime set out in Article 9 has been committed

shall, if it has reason to believe that an alleged offender has fled from its territory, communicate to the Secretary-General of the United Nations and, directly or through the Secretary-General, to the State or States concerned all the pertinent facts regarding the crime committed and all available information regarding the identity of the alleged offender.

2. Whenever a crime set out in Article 9 has been committed, any State Party which has information concerning the victim and circumstances of the crime shall endeavour to transmit such information, under the conditions provided for in its national law, fully and promptly to the Secretary-General of the United Nations and the State or States concerned.

Article 13
Measures to ensure prosecution or extradition

1. Where the circumstances so warrant, the State Party in whose territory the alleged offender is present shall take the appropriate measures under its national law to ensure that person's presence for the purpose of prosecution or extradition.

2. Measures taken in accordance with paragraph 1 shall be notified, in conformity with national law and without delay, to the Secretary-General of the United Nations and, either directly or through the Secretary-General, to:

(*a*)   The State where the crime was committed;

(*b*)   The State or States of which the alleged offender is a national or, if such person is a stateless person, in whose territory that person has his or her habitual residence;

(*c*)   The State or States of which the victim is a national; and

(*d*)   Other interested States.

Article 14
Prosecution of alleged offenders

The State Party in whose territory the alleged offender is present

249

shall, if it does not extradite that person, submit, without exception whatsoever and without undue delay, the case to its competent authorities for the purpose of prosecution, through proceedings in accordance with the law of that State. Those authorities shall take their decision in the same manner as in the case of an ordinary offence of a grave nature under the law of that State.

Article 15
Extradition of alleged offenders

1. To the extent that the crimes set out in Article 9 are not extraditable offences in any extradition treaty existing between States Parties, they shall be deemed to be included as such therein. States Parties undertake to include those crimes as extraditable offences in every extradition treaty to be concluded between them.

2. If a State Party which makes extradition conditional on the existence of a treaty receives a request for extradition from another State Party with which it has no extradition treaty, it may at its option consider this Convention as the legal basis for extradition in respect of those crimes. Extradition shall be subject to the conditions provided in the law of the requested State.

3. States Parties which do not make extradition conditional on the existence of a treaty shall recognize those crimes as extraditable offences between themselves subject to the conditions provided in the law of the requested State.

4. Each of those crimes shall be treated, for the purposes of extradition between States Parties, as if it had been committed not only in the place in which it occurred but also in the territories of the States Parties which have established their jurisdiction in accordance with paragraph 1 or 2 of Article 10.

Article 16
Mutual assistance in criminal matters

1. States Parties shall afford one another the greatest measure of assistance in connection with criminal proceedings brought in respect of the crimes set out in Article 9, including assistance in obtaining evidence

at their disposal necessary for the proceedings. The law of the requested State shall apply in all cases.

2. The provisions of paragraph 1 shall not affect obligations concerning mutual assistance embodied in any other treaty.

Article 17
Fair treatment

1. Any person regarding whom investigations or proceedings are being carried out in connection with any of the crimes set out in Article 9 shall be guaranteed fair treatment, a fair trial and full protection of his or her rights at all stages of the investigations or proceedings.

2. Any alleged offender shall be entitled:

(*a*)   To communicate without delay with the nearest appropriate representative of the State or States of which such person is a national or which is otherwise entitled to protect that person's rights or, if such person is a stateless person, of the State which, at that person's request, is willing to protect that person's rights; and

(*b*)   To be visited by a representative of that State or those States.

Article 18
Notification of outcome of proceedings

The State Party where an alleged offender is prosecuted shall communicate the final outcome of the proceedings to the Secretary-General of the United Nations, who shall transmit the information to other States Parties.

Article 19
Dissemination

The States Parties undertake to disseminate this Convention as widely as possible and, in particular, to include the study thereof, as well as relevant provisions of international humanitarian law, in their programmes of military instruction.

Article 20
Savings clauses

Nothing in this Convention shall affect:

(a) The applicability of international humanitarian law and universally recognized standards of human rights as contained in international instruments in relation to the protection of United Nations operations and United Nations and associated personnel or the responsibility of such personnel to respect such law and standards;

(b) The rights and obligations of States, consistent with the Charter of the United Nations, regarding the consent to entry of persons into their territories;

(c) The obligation of United Nations and associated personnel to act in accordance with the terms of the mandate of a United Nations operation;

(d) The right of States which voluntarily contribute personnel to a United Nations operation to withdraw their personnel from participation in such operation; or

(e) The entitlement to appropriate compensation payable in the event of death, disability, injury or illness attributable to peace-keeping service by persons voluntarily contributed by States to United Nations operations.

Article 21
Right of self-defence

Nothing in this Convention shall be construed so as to derogate from the right to act in self-defence.

Article 22
Dispute settlement

1. Any dispute between two or more States Parties concerning the interpretation or application of this Convention which is not settled by

negotiation shall, at the request of one of them, be submitted to arbitration. If within six months from the date of the request for arbitration the parties are unable to agree on the organization of the arbitration, any one of those parties may refer the dispute to the International Court of Justice by application in conformity with the Statute of the Court.

2. Each State Party may at the time of signature, ratification, acceptance or approval of this Convention or accession thereto declare that it does not consider itself bound by all or part of paragraph 1. The other States Parties shall not be bound by paragraph 1 or the relevant part thereof with respect to any State Party which has made such a reservation.

3. Any State Party which has made a reservation in accordance with paragraph 2 may at any time withdraw that reservation by notification to the Secretary-General of the United Nations.

Article 23
Review meetings

At the request of one or more States Parties, and if approved by a majority of States Parties, the Secretary-General of the United Nations shall convene a meeting of the States Parties to review the implementation of the Convention, and any problems encountered with regard to its application.

Article 24
Signature

This Convention shall be open for signature by all States, until 31 December 1995, at United Nations Headquarters in New York.

Article 25
Ratification, acceptance or approval

This Convention is subject to ratification, acceptance or approval. Instruments of ratification, acceptance or approval shall be deposited with the Secretary-General of the United Nations.

Article 26
Accession

This Convention shall be open for accession by any State. The instruments of accession shall be deposited with the Secretary-General of the United Nations.

Article 27
Entry into force

1. This Convention shall enter into force thirty days after twenty-two instruments of ratification, acceptance, approval or accession have been deposited with the Secretary-General of the United Nations.

2. For each State ratifying, accepting, approving or acceding to the Convention after the deposit of the twenty-second instrument of ratification, acceptance, approval or accession, the Convention shall enter into force on the thirtieth day after the deposit by such State of its instrument of ratification, acceptance, approval or accession.

Article 28
Denunciation

1. A State Party may denounce this Convention by written notification to the Secretary-General of the United Nations.

2. Denunciation shall take effect one year following the date on which notification is received by the Secretary-General of the United Nations.

Article 29
Authentic texts

The original of this Convention, of which the Arabic, Chinese, English, French, Russian and Spanish texts are equally authentic, shall be deposited with the Secretary-General of the United Nations, who shall send certified copies thereof to all States.

---

23. Geneva Convention for the Amelioration of the Condition of the Wounded and Sick in Armed Forces in the Field (selected excerpts)

Signed at Geneva on 12 August 1949
In force on 21 October 1950
United Nations, Treaty Series, vol. 75, No. 970
Depositary: Swiss Federal Council

...

CHAPTER I
GENERAL PROVISIONS

...

Article 3

In the case of armed conflict not of an international character occurring in the territory of one of the High Contracting Parties, each Party to the conflict shall be bound to apply, as a minimum, the following provisions:

1. Persons taking no active part in the hostilities, including members of armed forces who have laid down their arms and those placed *hors de combat* by sickness, wounds, detention, or any other cause, shall in all circumstances be treated humanely, without any adverse distinction founded on race, colour, religion or faith, sex, birth or wealth, or any other similar criteria.

To this end, the following acts are and shall remain prohibited at any time and in any place whatsoever with respect to the above-mentioned persons:

...

(b)   taking of hostages;

24. Geneva Convention for the Amelioration of the Condition of Wounded, Sick and Shipwrecked Members of Armed Forces at Sea (selected excerpts)

Signed at Geneva on 12 August 1949
In force on 21 October 1950
United Nations, Treaty Series, vol. 75, No. 971
Depositary: Swiss Federal Council

...

CHAPTER I
GENERAL PROVISIONS

...

Article 3

In the case of armed conflict not of an international character occurring in the territory of one of the High Contracting Parties, each Party to the conflict shall be bound to apply, as a minimum, the following provisions:

1. Persons taking no active part in the hostilities, including members of armed forces who have laid down their arms and those placed *hors de combat* by sickness, wounds, detention, or any other cause, shall in all circumstances be treated humanely, without any adverse distinction founded on race, colour, religion or faith, sex, birth or wealth, or any other similar criteria.

To this end, the following acts are and shall remain prohibited at any time and in any place whatsoever with respect to the above-mentioned persons:

...

    (*b*)   taking of hostages;

25. Geneva Convention Relative to the Treatment of Prisoners of War (selected excerpts)

Signed at Geneva on 12 August 1949
In force on 21 October 1950
United Nations, Treaty Series, vol. 75, No. 972
Depositary: Swiss Federal Council

...

PART I
GENERAL PROVISIONS

...

Article 3

In the case of armed conflict not of an international character occurring in the territory of one of the High Contracting Parties, each Party to the conflict shall be bound to apply, as a minimum, the following provisions:

1. Persons taking no active part in the hostilities, including members of armed forces who have laid down their arms and those placed *hors de combat* by sickness, wounds, detention, or any other cause, shall in all circumstances be treated humanely, without any adverse distinction founded on race, colour, religion or faith, sex, birth or wealth, or any other similar criteria.

To this end the following acts are and shall remain prohibited at any time and in any place whatsoever with respect to the above-mentioned persons:

...

(*b*)   taking of hostages;

26. Geneva Convention Relative to the Protection of Civilian Persons in Time of War (selected excerpts)

Signed at Geneva on 12 August 1949
In force on 21 October 1950
United Nations, Treaty Series, vol. 75, No. 973
Depositary: Swiss Federal Council

...

PART I
GENERAL PROVISIONS

...

Article 3

In the case of armed conflict not of an international character occurring in the territory of one of the High Contracting Parties, each Party to the conflict shall be bound to apply, as a minimum, the following provisions:

1. Persons taking no active part in the hostilities, including members of armed forces who have laid down their arms and those placed *hors de combat* by sickness, wounds, detention, or any other cause, shall in all circumstances be treated humanely, without any adverse distinction founded on race, colour, religion or faith, sex, birth or wealth, or any other similar criteria.

To this end the following acts are and shall remain prohibited at any time and in any place whatsoever with respect to the above-mentioned persons:

...

(*b*)   taking of hostages;

...

PART III
STATUS AND TREATMENT OF PROTECTED PERSONS

SECTION I
PROVISIONS COMMON TO THE TERRITORIES
OF THE PARTIES TO THE CONFLICT
AND TO OCCUPIED TERRITORIES

...

Article 33

No protected person may be punished for an offence he or she has not personally committed. Collective penalties and likewise all measures of intimidation or of terrorism are prohibited.

Pillage is prohibited.

Reprisals against protected persons and their property are prohibited.

Article 34

The taking of hostages is prohibited.

...

PART IV
EXECUTION OF THE CONVENTION

SECTION I
GENERAL PROVISIONS

...

Article 146

The High Contracting Parties undertake to enact any legislation necessary to provide effective penal sanctions for persons committing, or ordering to be committed, any of the grave breaches of the present Convention defined in the following Article.

Each High Contracting Party shall be under the obligation to search for persons alleged to have committed, or to have ordered to be committed, such grave breaches, and shall bring such persons, regardless of their nationality, before its own courts. It may also, if it prefers, and in accordance with the provisions of its own legislation, hand such persons over for trial to another High Contracting Party concerned, provided such High Contracting Party has made out a *prima facie* case.

Each High Contracting Party shall take measures necessary for the suppression of all acts contrary to the provisions of the present Convention other than the grave breaches defined in the following Article.

In all circumstances, the accused persons shall benefit by safeguards of proper trial and defence, which shall not be less favourable than those provided by Article 105 and those following of the Geneva Convention relative to the Treatment of Prisoners of War of 12 August 1949.

Article 147

Grave breaches to which the preceding Article relates shall be those involving any of the following acts, if committed against persons or property protected by the present Convention: wilful killing, torture or inhuman treatment, including biological experiments, wilfully causing great suffering or serious injury to body or health, unlawful deportation or transfer or unlawful confinement of a protected person, compelling a protected person to serve in the forces of a hostile Power, or wilfully depriving a protected person of the rights of fair and regular trial prescribed in the present Convention, taking of hostages and extensive destruction and appropriation of property, not justified by military necessity and carried out unlawfully and wantonly.

27. Protocol Additional to the Geneva Conventions of 12 August 1949, and Relating to the Protection of Victims of International Armed Conflicts (Protocol I) (selected excerpts)

Signed at Geneva on 8 June 1977
In force on 7 December 1978
United Nations, Treaty Series, vol. 1125, No. 17512
Depositary: Swiss Federal Council

....

PART III
METHODS AND MEANS OF WARFARE
COMBATANT AND PRISONER-OF-WAR STATUS

...

SECTION II
COMBATANT AND PRISONER-OF-WAR STATUS

Article 43
Armed forces

1. The armed forces of a Party to a conflict consist of all organized armed forces, groups and units which are under a command responsible to that Party for the conduct or its subordinates, even if that Party is represented by a government or an authority not recognized by an adverse Party. Such armed forces shall be subject to an internal disciplinary system which, *inter alia*, shall enforce compliance with the rules of international law applicable in armed conflict.

...

Article 44
Combatants and prisoners of war

...

2. While all combatants are obliged to comply with the rules of international law applicable in armed conflict, violations of these rules shall not deprive a combatant of his right to be a combatant or, if he falls into the power of an adverse Party, of his right to be a prisoner of war, except as provided in paragraphs 3 and 4.

...

PART IV
CIVILIAN POPULATION

SECTION I
GENERAL PROTECTION AGAINST EFFECTS OF HOSTILITIES

...

CHAPTER II
CIVILIANS AND CIVILIAN POPULATION

...

Article 51
Protection of the civilian population

...

2. The civilian population as such, as well as individual civilians, shall not be the object of attack. Acts or threats of violence the primary purpose of which is to spread terror among the civilian population are prohibited.

...

SECTION III
TREATMENT OF PERSONS IN THE
POWER OF A PARTY TO THE CONFLICT

CHAPTER I
FIELD OF APPLICATION AND PROTECTION
OF PERSONS AND OBJECTS

...

Article 75
Fundamental guarantees

...

2. The following acts are and shall remain prohibited at any time and in any place whatsoever, whether committed by civilian or by military agents:

...

(*c*)   the taking of hostages;

...

PART V
EXECUTION OF THE CONVENTIONS
AND OF THIS PROTOCOL

...

SECTION II
REPRESSION OF BREACHES OF THE CONVENTIONS
AND OF THIS PROTOCOL

Article 85
Repression of breaches of this Protocol

...

2. Acts described as grave breaches in the Conventions are grave breaches of this Protocol if committed against persons in the power of an adverse Party protected by Articles 44, 45 and 73 of this Protocol, or against the wounded, sick and shipwrecked of the adverse Party who are protected by this Protocol, or against those medical or religious personnel,

medical units or medical transports which are under the control of the adverse Party and are protected by this Protocol.

...

28. Protocol Additional to the Geneva Conventions of 12 August 1949, and Relating to the Protection of Victims of Non-international Armed Conflicts (Protocol II) (selected excerpts)

Signed at Geneva on 8 June 1977
In force on 7 December 1978
United Nations, Treaty Series, vol. 1125, No. 17513
Depositary: Swiss Federal Council

....

PART II
HUMANE TREATMENT

Article 4
Fundamental guarantees

...

2. Without prejudice to the generality of the foregoing, the following acts against the persons referred to in paragraph 1 are and shall remain prohibited at any time and in any place whatsoever:

...

(*c*)   taking of hostages;

(*d*)   acts of terrorism;

...

PART IV
CIVILIAN POPULATION

Article 13
Protection of the civilian population

...

2. The civilian population as such, as well as individual civilians, shall not be the object of attack. Acts or threats of violence the primary purpose of which is to spread terror among the civilian population are prohibited.

...

Litho in United Nations, New York
20637—January 2001—2,810
ISBN 92-1-133631-7

United Nations publication
Sales No. E.01.V.3
ST/ESA/269